Why I Don't Work Here Anymore

Anymore

A Leader's Guide to Offset
the Financial and Emotional Costs
of Toxic Employees

Why I Don't Work Here Anymore

A Leader's Guide to Offset the Financial and Emotional Costs of Toxic Employees

Dr. Mitchell Kusy

CRC Press
Taylor & Francis Group
Boca Raton London New York

CRC Press is an imprint of the
Taylor & Francis Group, an **informa** business

A PRODUCTIVITY PRESS BOOK

CRC Press
Taylor & Francis Group
6000 Broken Sound Parkway NW, Suite 300
Boca Raton, FL 33487-2742

International Standard Book Number-13: 978-1-138-30326-3 (Paperback)
International Standard Book Number-13: 978-0-203-73124-6 (eBook)

**Visit the Taylor & Francis Web site at
http://www.taylorandfrancis.com**

**and the CRC Press Web site at
http://www.crcpress.com**

Contents

Preface ix
Acknowledgments xi
Author xiii

Chapter 1   Evidence-Based Insights about Toxic Behaviors 1

A Definition and Three Categories of Toxic Behaviors 5
Hard Data That Become a Call to Action 6
Understanding Toxic People Who Are High Performers 9
Bullying in the Context of Toxic Behaviors 9
Are *You* a Toxic Person? 11
The Power of the Apology 13

Chapter 2   Myths about Toxic Behaviors 17

Myth #1: You Can't Calculate the Financial Cost
of Toxic People 17
Myth #2: Many Toxic People Are Incompetent 24
Myth #3: Ignoring the Toxic Person Will Stop
the Behavior 25
Myth #4: Concrete Feedback Will Handle Their
Manipulations 27
Myth #5: Making Up Your Mind You Won't Put Up
with Toxic Behaviors Is Enough 29
Myth #6: There's Little You Can Do If Your Boss Is Toxic ... 31
Myth #7: Keeping the Problem to Yourself Will Protect
You in the Long Run 32

Chapter 3   Powerful Ways to Give Toxic People Feedback 35

Cost-Benefit Strategy 36
Direct Report Strategy 38
Peer Strategy 42
The Boss Strategy 44
Mixing and Matching Your Strategies 48

Chapter 4 How We Enable Toxic Behaviors to Persist 53

Toxic Protectors and Toxic Buffers 53
Are You a Toxic Protector? 56
Are You a Toxic Buffer? 56
What to Do If You Are a Toxic Protector or Buffer 59
What to Do If Someone Else Is a Toxic Protector
or Buffer 60
Getting Out of Being Stuck 63

Chapter 5 Hiring and Exiting Practices That Address Toxic
Behaviors.. 65

A Poorly Managed Recruiting Process.................................... 66
The Recruiting Cue Sheet 67
The Danger of Hypothetical Questions....................................69
Analyzing Responses from Candidate Interviews..................71
Vary Your Interviewing Questions 73
Check References the Right Way...74
When Traditional Exit Interviews Do Not Work 75

Chapter 6 Failures and Triumphs of Performance
Management in the Toxic World...................................... 79

Values Integration as an Antidote to Toxic Behaviors 80
Three Powerful Performance Management Practices...........81
A Performance Management Template....................................83
The 70-30 Split Performance Model...85
Protocol for Firing the Toxic Person...................................... 86

Chapter 7 A Powerful Team Assessment Method 89

Case Simulation of the Campbell-Hallam Team
Development Survey™ 94
What Happens When the Team Leader Is Toxic 99
How to Best Engage the Campbell-Hallam Team
Development Survey™ 101
Differences Between the Campbell-Hallam Team
Development Survey™ and Traditional Culture
Assessment Tools..102

Chapter 8 Remain Vigilant 103

Are Your One-on-One Meetings Really Enough? 103
Skip-Level Discussions..104
Case Example of a Skip-Level Conversation.........................106
Comparing the Skip-Level Discussion with 360-Degree
Feedback 109

Chapter 9 How to Build a Culture of Everyday Civility 113

The Problem, the Action, and the Expected Outcome........ 113
Prioritizing Your Actions 115
Obstacles That Can Get in the Way of Action.....................117
Building a Culture of Everyday Civility One Action
at a Time..118

References... 119

Index.. 121

Preface

If you are like most people, you have experienced the emotional impact of toxic people. As you will discover in this book, almost no one has been immune to the devastation they have wreaked on individuals, teams, and organizations. Including this author.

The unique perspectives of this book incorporate evidence-based studies conducted by a myriad of researchers, including the national study that I have conducted with my co-researcher, Dr. Elizabeth Holloway. And beyond these studies, I believe you will discover how to handle these individuals through the many templates, assessment inventories, and case scenarios I have included in this book.

I wish I had these strategies when I worked with one uncivil individual who was the key catalyst in my leaving a wonderful position. During the course of research others and I have conducted, I discovered I was not alone. While others also experienced the turmoil of working with a toxic person, many shared experiences of how this impacted their emotional well-being and organizational resources.

In my work with thousands of leaders—helping them deal with the damage these individuals bring to organizations—I have found two missing gaps. First, leaders have not had evidence-based models with which to handle these disruptive individuals. Second, leaders have not had at their ready the research needed to feel confident in their actions to address uncivil employees. With this book, they now have both.

Beyond understanding and dealing with toxic behaviors, I hope you will find this book a positive draw for how to design organizational and team cultures of everyday civility. This is the best way for leaders to posture respectful engagement as the mantra for all. Please enjoy and use my book!

Mitch Kusy

Acknowledgments

I would like to personally acknowledge five individuals who have made this book possible. My life partner of over 30 years, Scott Vrchota, has been not only the source of enduring encouragement but also the person whose insight led to this book's marvelous title. Your love and support continually go noticed with deep appreciation.

To my very close friend, Brad Fagerstrom, who, along with Scott, has helped me design a change formula to understand the financial impact of toxic individuals—I have deep gratitude for your wisdom and the gift of your friendship.

And to my dear friend, Dr. Elizabeth Holloway, with whom I have conducted the seminal research study on toxic people and co-authored *Toxic Workplace! Managing Toxic Personalities and Their Systems of Power.* Without you, there would have been no research study and no first book.

To Laurie Harper, who, as my wise agent, has been there with me from the inception of this book's germ of an idea to the final rollout of the book's proposal. I thank you.

Finally, I extend my sincere gratitude to my colleague, the renowned Dr. Alan Rosenstein, whose pioneering and seminal research in disruptive behaviors in healthcare has led me to better understand their impact and resolution.

Author

Dr. Mitchell Kusy, a 2005 Fulbright Scholar in organization development, is professor of organization learning and development at the Graduate School of Leadership & Change at Antioch University in Yellow Springs, Ohio, with campuses in Los Angeles and Santa Barbara, California; Keene, New Hampshire; and Seattle, Washington. A registered organization development consultant, Mitch has consulted with hundreds of organizations nationally and internationally; he has been a keynote speaker around the globe. Mitch has helped create organizational communities of respectful engagement, facilitated large-scale systems to successful change, and engaged teams through assessment and team-designed actions—all with a focus on improving organizational culture and long-term return on investment. He previously headed organization development for HealthPartners and the leadership development area for American Express Financial Advisors. Before his leadership in national and international organizations, Mitch was a full professor at the University of St. Thomas, Minneapolis, where he co-designed the doctoral program in organization development. Previous to *Why I Don't Work Here Anymore*, Mitch co-authored five business books. In 1998, he received the Minnesota Organization Development Practitioner of the Year Award. He resides in Minneapolis and Palm Springs, and may be contacted at mitchellkusy@gmail.com or through his website at www.mitchellkusy.com.

1

Evidence-Based Insights about Toxic Behaviors

You have likely heard stories from friends, family members, and colleagues who quit a great job because of a single, uncivil individual. Likely described to you with such adjectives as shaming, passive-aggressive, and humiliating, this person may have had other terms attributed to his/her behavior. And probably this individual received the label of "toxic." What you may not realize is that beyond their emotional abuse, toxic people impact the financial outcomes of any organization. This book will provide significant research and cases about this dual impact to our emotions and to an organization's finances—and what you can do about it.

Beyond these stories of others, the research presented will likely demonstrate that *you* have been affected by toxic people in the course of your own career. I know I have. You see, I resigned from a great position because of a toxic colleague. When I gave my boss official notice, she tried to talk me out of my decision. Because I had stellar performance reviews, she could not understand why I was resigning. I gave her a fictitious reason because I knew she would not believe me since my uncivil peer was also a star—albeit toxic—and the cause of others leaving as well. Because of his "star status," his behavior was not on my boss's radar screen. Unfortunately, this is not unusual. Many toxic people are chameleons—very capable of "knocking down and kissing up." That is how my toxic colleague escaped detection. And as you will discover in this book, how many toxic people get away with bad behavior.

In my research and work in helping leaders deal with this scourge, I found that I am not alone. More people have had to deal with toxic behaviors than many imagine. But rather than rely solely on my personal experiences, this book will review the research in this arena. Figure 1.1 shows

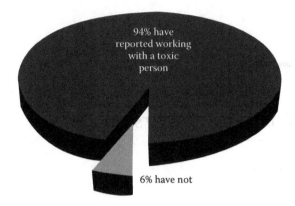

FIGURE 1.1

Research demonstrates that 94% of over 400 leaders stated they have worked within a five-year period with a toxic person (Kusy & Holloway, 2009).

the alarming statistic of the percentage of over 400 leaders who stated they have worked with a toxic person within a five-year period (Kusy & Holloway, 2009).

It is reasonable to conclude, then, that most people in leadership positions understand the devastation toxic people can cause for teams and organizations. However, many do not! And so that's why this book is here. *Why I Don't Work Here Anymore* will outline and help you understand the devastation caused to anyone who gets in the path of toxic people, as well as apply the most successful approaches for managing them and the situations they create. This understanding and these concomitant strategies will help leaders offset the emotional and financial costs brought on by these behaviors.

But I am getting ahead of myself. Let's take a step back. What *is* a toxic person? These are people who demonstrate disrespectful, uncivil behavior resulting in wide-ranging effects to our psyches, individual and team performances, *and* the bottom line. They are bullies, narcissists, manipulators, and control freaks; they're people who shame, humiliate, belittle, or take credit for the work of others.

> Toxic people demonstrate disrespectful, uncivil behavior with wide-ranging effects to our psyches, individual and team performances, *and* the bottom line. They are bullies, narcissists, manipulators, and control freaks; they're people who shame, humiliate, belittle, or take credit for the work of others.

In the several years since I began working with Dr. Elizabeth Holloway to study and then help hundreds of organizations deal with this problem, I have come to three overall conclusions:

- These individuals cost an organization time, money, valuable employees, and emotional health.
- Many organizations do not recognize this as a significant problem.
- Many leaders do not know how to handle this in the most effective ways possible.

A toxic person's incivility can be contagious, spreading her/his venom so that others sometimes respond in toxic ways as well. So why not just fire the person? Firing is often the last resort in many organizations because these people are clever chameleons—very capable of "knocking down and kissing up." They shrewdly disguise their behaviors by demonstrating countervailing behaviors like showing their boss how their demanding behaviors are working effectively to increase performance; the boss then interprets these behaviors as "tough, precise, and needed." Unfortunately, this increase in performance may be short-term as targets of the incivility are likely to quit, or at least reduce their performance. Simultaneously, toxic individuals also kick down below them in ways that can be manipulative, condescending, shaming, and bullying. Unfortunately, firing them is easier said than done, especially when these people are perceived as productive. Who wants to fire someone who has outstanding performance? *You* do, because their behavior derails others while they are employed *and* even after they're gone. Table 1.1 provides some of the features of toxic individuals who are chameleons that "knock down and kiss up."

TABLE 1.1

Some of the Features of Toxic Chameleons Who "Knock Down and Kiss Up"

- Gives the boss what the boss wants to hear
- Is uncivil to direct reports, but is gracious to the boss
- Presents overly harsh criticism to others when outside the view of the boss
- Explains to the boss that he/she has very high expectations but demonstrates these expectations to others with unrealistic demands

In this book, you will discover not only *how* to best fire these individuals, but also how to take a proactive stance that may preclude you from having to fire them. Whether to fire or not is just one of the many questions I'll cover.

One of my clients shared this scenario with me:

> Our CEO has temper tantrums. The board thinks he walks on water, but they have no clue what's going on. One time I even saw this guy kick the conference-room table leg so hard in an angry outburst that the water pitcher fell over. What's amazing to me is that the board doesn't attribute the vast number of people exiting the company to *him*. Those who have quit have not only been his direct reports but also others who have had to deal with this guy on a regular basis. What a fiasco!

Many uncivil individuals strike a careful balance with two competing workplace personas, Dr. Jekyll and Mr. Hyde. It takes deliberate methods and careful attention to uncover this duplicity. Those in power positions often see Dr. Jekyll, while peers and direct reports must cope with the ravages of Mr. Hyde. Essentially, these people are winning the battle of perception. Anyone who brings up having difficulty with Mr. Hyde may be labeled a complainer, a nuisance, a non-team player, or worse—someone who is not committed to the organization. It is quite understandable, then, that only 6 percent of targets of incivility endured the behavior "often" or "many times" (Cortina, Magley, Williams, & Langhout, 2001). This makes getting your hands around these behaviors even more difficult. But it can be done.

> Many uncivil individuals strike a careful balance with two competing workplace personas, Dr. Jekyll and Mr. Hyde. It takes deliberate methods and careful attention to uncover this duplicity. Those in power positions often see Dr. Jekyll, while peers and direct reports must cope with the ravages of Mr. Hyde. Essentially, these people are winning the battle of perception.

Why I Don't Work Here Anymore will address both proactive and reactive strategies for leaders. Proactive intervention focuses on how not to allow toxic people to get away with uncivil behaviors *before* the behaviors escalate. Reactive strategies position leaders to take action *after* devastation has hit.

A DEFINITION AND THREE CATEGORIES OF TOXIC BEHAVIORS

As a result of our research study, we have defined these individuals as anyone demonstrating a pattern of inappropriate and disruptive actions that seriously debilitate individuals, teams, and/or organizations over the long term (Kusy & Holloway, 2009). Their uncivil venom stings the same *whatever* we call them.

Their behaviors emanate from three primary domains (Kusy & Holloway, 2009):

- Shaming
- Passive hostility
- Sabotage

Some shaming behavior includes humiliating others one-on-one or in public, as well as taking special delight in pointing out the mistakes of co-workers, dressing someone down, bullying, and giving condescending feedback for the sake of being overly righteous. Passive hostility includes what is often referred to as "passive-aggressive" behavior—getting one's anger out in "crooked" ways like taking pot shots at someone, being overly sarcastic with the intent of hurting, spreading malicious rumors, and "backstabbing" by not sharing an issue directly with someone but mentioning it to others with the intent of maligning someone's reputation. Sabotage includes such behaviors as seeking retaliation and meddling in order to bring down a team or individuals out of self-interest. Some of these behaviors transcend across all three domains—these include yelling and verbal abuse, rudeness, and teasing that stings. Table 1.2 summarizes some of the main behaviors within each domain.

TABLE 1.2

Three Domains of Toxic Behaviors (Kusy & Holloway, 2009)

- *Shaming:* Humiliation, needlessly pointing out mistakes, condescending feedback for the sake of being righteous
- *Passive hostility:* Passive-aggressive behavior, taking "pot shots," overly sarcastic with the intent of hurting, spreading rumors, "backstabbing"
- *Sabotage:* Seeking retaliation, meddling in order to bring down the team or individual because of the person's own self-interests

These three domains of behavior emanate from overall disrespect and incivility that carry serious consequences for performance, and the bottom line.

> Three domains of toxic behavior—shaming, passive hostility, and sabotage—emanate from overall disrespect and incivility that carry serious consequences for people, performance, and the bottom line.

Now that you have some running definitions and descriptions, let's talk about what makes *Why I Don't Work Here Anymore* different from the dozens of other books on narcissists, egomaniacs, and toxic individuals. In this book, each of the chapters is focused on one clearly defined problem—with targeted leadership strategies to counter these problems in evidence-based ways. You will see the evidence displayed in the myriad of statistics I present from various research studies. I do not base these strategies on any form of intuition of what I think *might* work. Instead, I take the best of what the research has to offer, as well as what leading experts have found to be successful, and provide a cohesive plan of action. There may be some strategies that are easy to implement; others will be more difficult. You can decide for your own situation what is doable now, what may be doable with some additional support, and what can be delayed for a period of time.

HARD DATA THAT BECOME A CALL TO ACTION

Consider the following. Our research discovered that 51 percent of individuals who were the targets of these bad behaviors said they would quit (Kusy & Holloway, 2009). In another study, it was reported that 12 percent did quit (Pearson & Porath, 2009). In the healthcare setting, 24 percent of 1,121 respondents reported that they actually knew of a nurse who quit as a result of these disruptive behaviors (Rosenstein, 2002). And when you combine these statistics with human resource metrics demonstrating the cost of rehiring employees to replace those who quit, the financial outcome is astounding:

- For entry-level employees, replacement costs range from 30 to 50 percent of the annual salary for that employee;
- For mid-level employees, replacement costs are 150-plus percent of annual salary;
- And for high-level, specialized employees, costs are 400 percent of annual salary (Borysenko, 2015).

There are several ways to interpret these statistics. Since we know that many outstanding employees quit as a result of working with a toxic person, you need to do everything possible to make sure they do not. It is not usually about convincing them to stay. Rather, it is more about not allowing toxic people to get away with bad behavior. It is expensive to replace the outstanding individuals who quit as a result of one uncivil person, as these statistics demonstrate. Moreover, if the person has been productive, it is going to be difficult to replace their high performance—at least immediately. So, it is incumbent on leaders to do everything possible to take care of the situation proactively, before it gets out of hand and they have to deal with the deleterious effects these statistics demonstrate.

Consider some specifics within the healthcare industry, a field that has probably done more than any other to address toxic behaviors, which they often refer to as "disruptive." You may find the following statistics hard to swallow, but these have been demonstrated in dozens of studies. You may even have a renewed perspective the next time you visit your doctor or hospital.

Alan Rosenstein, MD, and Michelle O'Daniel are leading researchers and experts in reporting the devastation of disruptive behaviors in healthcare. They have established key links between disruptive behavior and patient safety. For example, in a study of 4530 participants (Rosenstein & O'Daniel, 2008), they found that a whopping 71 percent said that there was a significant association between disruptive behaviors of professionals and medical errors. And 27 percent saw this link leading to patient mortality. Finally, 75 percent said that these medical errors and subsequent patient deaths could have been prevented. Some of the behaviors Rosenstein and O'Daniel identified were intimidation, hostility, fear, lack of respect, passive-aggressive behaviors, and undermining others— all toxic behaviors as defined in this book. Table 1.3 provides a summary of these alarming statistics.

In a recent keynote address I delivered to a nonhealthcare leadership group, I brought up these healthcare statistics because we all receive

TABLE 1.3

Summary of the *Impact of Disruptive Behaviors in Healthcare* Based on the Research of Rosenstein & O'Daniel (2008)

- 71%: Saw an association between disruptive behaviors and patient safety
- 27%: Believed there was an association between these behaviors and patient mortality
- 75%: Said the medical errors could have been prevented

healthcare services at one time or another—and should be concerned, if not alarmed, by these troubling data. A gentleman raised his hand and spoke. "My wife is a nurse and has been continuously intimidated by a physician. So intimidated and fearful that when she questioned the medication order, rather than go to the physician issuing the order, she went to three colleagues to interpret it!" Fortunately, it was interpreted correctly. The bottom line: toxic behaviors—as demonstrated in this scenario by severe intimidation—can have serious ramifications, and depending on your field, those ramifications could deeply affect people's lives.

When we asked 400 leaders about how toxic the individual was that they were thinking about in our survey, 92 percent said it ranged from 7 to 10 on a scale of 1 to 10 (Kusy & Holloway, 2009). This is pretty revealing in terms of the pain and suffering this causes people at work.

Consider other hardline statistics that may have you thinking further about toxic behaviors. Several large-scale studies reported significant declines in performance for those who are the target of toxic people. Figure 1.2 provides evidence that when a customer witnessed an employee being rude towards another employee, 92% spoke negatively about the organization to others (Porath, MacInnis, & Folkes, 2011). And even more revealing: it didn't matter if the rudeness was directed at them or another employee! Do you want toxic people to have this kind of power?

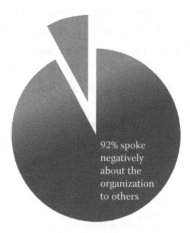

FIGURE 1.2

Customer response to witnessing an employee demonstrating uncivil behavior toward another employee (Porath et al., 2011).

UNDERSTANDING TOXIC PEOPLE
WHO ARE HIGH PERFORMERS

Many toxic individuals are high performers, and are sometimes even perfectionists. This can riddle an organization with spiraling negative effects. Here's a real case that demonstrates what happens when perfectionism is carried too far. One of my client groups was the executive team in a large medical center with multiple specialties. The chief medical officer on this team asked me how to cope with one particular surgeon who was creating havoc with her intimidating behavior—rousing many to fear her even when she was only passing by. I spent some time coaching this surgeon about the impact of her behavior, and her response surprised me. She quipped, "Would you want to go to a surgeon who was not perfect?"

This caused me to pause and reflect for a few brief moments, and I asked her a question in response: "If you were about to make a mistake in the operating suite, would you prefer to have someone call you on it or would you prefer to go on with your procedure because no one wanted to be a target of your wrath?" Silence. After this, she was much more amenable to coaching and to actually changing her behavior. In fact, she apologized to her team and engaged in new, positive behaviors with this team. While she slipped at times to old behaviors, she did improve and team members said that she was much more approachable. More importantly, the team reported that they believed they provided better patient service by functioning more effectively together, rather than as a group of individuals fearful of the surgeon. In the long run, team performance in the surgery suite improved.

So, perfectionism in and of itself may have some value, to an extent, but when paired with intimidation, it is highly damaging and undoes any benefit of the perfectionism by decreasing the performance of others.

> Perfectionism in and of itself may have some value, to an extent, but when paired with intimidation, it is highly damaging and undoes any benefit of the perfectionism by decreasing the performance of others.

BULLYING IN THE CONTEXT OF TOXIC BEHAVIORS

There has been significant public press over the past several years about the impact that bullying has on our personal psyches and on others. There

TABLE 1.4

Careerbuilder.com Study (2011) of 5600 Full-Time Workers on Bullying

- My comments were dismissed or not acknowledged (43 percent)
- I was falsely accused of mistakes I didn't make (40 percent)
- I was harshly criticized (38 percent)
- I was forced into doing work that really wasn't my job (38 percent)
- Different standards and policies were used for me than other workers (37 percent)
- I was given mean looks (31 percent)
- Others gossiped about me (27 percent)
- My boss yelled at me in front of other coworkers (24 percent)
- Belittling comments were made about my work during meetings (23 percent)
- Someone else stole credit for my work (21 percent)

seems to be very little distinction, if any, between bullying and toxic behaviors. Consider the research identified in Table 1.4 from a recent study of bullying in the workplace (careerbuilder.com, 2011). In this study of 5600 full-time employees nationwide with percentages responding to each item in parentheses, you will hopefully see that bullying is just one form of toxic behaviors.

Any one of these items may be perceived as toxic. If you review the previous definition I have provided regarding toxic behaviors, these bullying behaviors align with this definition. Let's take a step back and analyze more specifically the previous definition of toxic behaviors. These are disrespectful, uncivil behaviors with wide-ranging effects on our psyches, individual and team performance, *and* the bottom line. Toxic people are bullies, narcissists, manipulators, and control freaks; they're people who shame, humiliate, belittle, or take credit for the work of others.

Breaking this definition down even further, the three categories of toxic behaviors we have found include shaming, passive hostility, and sabotage (Kusy & Holloway, 2009). Every item in the careerbuilder.com study falls into our definition and at least one of these three categories of toxic people.

An interesting exercise to further make sense of the items from the careerbuilder.com research would be to see which of these items fall into the three categories of toxic people: shaming, passive hostility, and sabotage. And rather than just doing this exercise solo, it could be insightful to do the exercise in a team format as identified in Table 1.5.

TABLE 1.5

Team Exercise to Align careerbuilder.com Items within the Three Categories of Toxic Behaviors

---

Within a team format, please consider each of the items from the careerbuilder.com study and see how these align with the three categories of toxic behaviors—shaming, passive hostility, and sabotage. To help further this assessment please consider the following:

1. Before your team meeting, please distribute these items electronically (without percentages) to team members and ask them to anonymously indicate those behaviors they have experienced in the past year
2. Collect the data on a sheet of paper without names to protect anonymity; identify the percentage of responses on each item
3. Share the data with the team and discuss:
   a. What are some examples of these behaviors they have experienced?
   b. How do you refer to these behaviors? Toxic? Bullying? Other?
   c. How did you intervene? Were these actions successful or not successful? Why or why not?
   d. Do we want to do something about the behaviors that are most troubling?

ARE *YOU* A TOXIC PERSON?

Now that you hopefully have a better feel for what constitutes toxic behavior, I issue you this question. Are you a toxic person? Here's a quiz for you to take to help you decide (Table 1.6).

As you process this information, please keep one important statistic in mind from our research study (Kusy & Holloway, 2009): many toxic individuals are clueless about the impact of their behavior on others. This quiz helps expose this cluelessness in two ways. First, it is designed to present you with concrete behaviors associated with toxic people. Second, it asks you to get a "second opinion." In comparing your responses with your trusted colleague, consider these thoughts that you might have:

- "I'm the only one who has the guts to do something about this."
- "Everyone else is afraid to speak up, so I do."
- "No one brings to the table what I bring."
- "The rest of the team is chicken to oppose this idea."

Many toxic individuals are clueless about the impact of their behavior on others.

TABLE 1.6

"Are You a Toxic Person?" Quiz

To help you determine if you should be concerned about being a toxic person, please color in the circle that corresponds best with your response to this next statement:

How characteristic of you are the following behaviors?

	Not Characteristic of Me	Somewhat Characteristic of Me	Highly Characteristic of Me
1. Have difficulty accepting negative feedback	◯	◯	◯
2. Shame people in group settings	◯	◯	◯
3. Shame people one-on-one	◯	◯	◯
4. Take "pot shots" at people in private	◯	◯	◯
5. Take "pot shots" at people in public	◯	◯	◯
6. Use my authority to punish	◯	◯	◯
7. Act disrespectfully with those I manage	◯	◯	◯
8. Act disrespectfully with peers	◯	◯	◯
9. "Put down" people with sarcasm	◯	◯	◯
10. Bully others	◯	◯	◯
11. Manipulate others to get what I want	◯	◯	◯
12. Am a control freak	◯	◯	◯
13. Take credit for the work of others	◯	◯	◯
14. Am more respectful to my boss than others	◯	◯	◯
15. Belittle others	◯	◯	◯
16. Provide needlessly harsh feedback	◯	◯	◯
17. Do not acknowledge others when I should	◯	◯	◯
18. Gossip about others to get back at the person	◯	◯	◯
19. Yell at someone in front of others	◯	◯	◯
20. Retaliate	◯	◯	◯

Instructions for interpreting results: The purpose of this quiz is to understand your own toxic behaviors. To assess this understanding:

1. Look down the list and see which behaviors cause you to pause and be concerned. Hold these thoughts.
2. Invite someone who knows you well and trusts you to complete this same quiz on you. This could be your peer, direct report, or boss—anyone who will provide accurate, honest feedback.
3. Compare responses.
4. Have an open discussion with this person.
5. Develop an action plan (if appropriate) after reading the remainder of this book. As relevant, engage this person in constructing this action plan.
6. Monitor results. Act as needed.

In reviewing these thought statements, it is important to separate what might be valid and what might be toxic. When are these well-intentioned thoughts likely to turn sour? For instance, consider the first one: "Have difficulty accepting negative feedback." This *could* be true. However, if this thinking is a pattern, you're more than likely *not* the only one able to do something about it. So, if any of these statements rings true for you, ask someone you trust about this. Since many toxic people are clueless about the impact of their behavior on others, it is important to get validation. If you have engaged in any of the behaviors in the quiz *and* want to do something about it, consider starting with an apology.

THE POWER OF THE APOLOGY

I discovered the power of the apology when I was doing research for one of my previous books, *Breaking the code of silence: Prominent leaders reveal how they rebounded from seven critical mistakes* (Kusy & Essex, 2005). In synthesizing the research from several sources including sociology, psychology, communications, and anthropology, I learned that most people in Western culture apologize incorrectly and, ultimately, ineffectively. Specifically, most individuals apologize with a "Yes, but" framework. Consider how you apologize. Does it sound like this? "I'm sorry, but…" Table 1.7 illustrates the flawed way many apologize in Western culture.

This two-step apology doesn't even come close to what an apology needs to be. Why? Because what comes after the "but" is often regarded as the excuse, which ends up essentially negating the apology. Instead, experts from such fields as psychology, sociology, anthropology, and theology have found what boils down to a four-step apology far more effective, as is demonstrated in Table 1.8.

So, now let's apply this four-step apology process to some of the behaviors that might stand out from the "Are you a toxic person?" quiz

TABLE 1.7

Flawed Apology Sequence

1. "I apologize (or "I'm sorry") for (behavior inserted here)."
2. "But, I was (insert the reason here)."

TABLE 1.8

Effective Apology Sequence

1. State what you did in concrete terms—framed in the past.
2. Acknowledge how this behavior has affected others.
3. Issue sorrow through an apology phrase.
4. Declare what you will do to rectify this situation in the future.

TABLE 1.9

Applying the "Four-Step" Apology When You Demonstrate Uncivil Behaviors

1. *State what you did in concrete terms, framed in the past.* "Over the past six months at our team meetings, I have been intimidating you through my bullying behavior in order for you to agree with me, hitting you over the head with statistics that I skewed in my own direction, and interrupting you at team meetings."
2. *Acknowledge how this behavior has affected another person or persons.* "I know this has resulted in your losing confidence in me as your team leader."
3. *Issue sorrow through an apology phrase.* "I apologize for this behavior. I am sorry I did this."
4. *Declare what you will do to rectify in the future.* "In the future, I will initiate some changes in my bullying behavior. To act on these changes most effectively, I would further like to ask for your support. Specifically, here's what I have in mind:
   • If I revert to my old intimidating behavior, you may interrupt me and call it to my attention at the meeting.
   • If you do not feel comfortable doing this at the meeting, you are welcome to come to me one-on-one and bring it to my attention."

(see Table 1.9). If, after taking the quiz (Table 1.6) you discover you might be a toxic person, take heed and apologize. And if you're not a toxic person but have one reporting to you, you can teach them this apology sequence.

Every step is important in this newly framed apology. Overlooking any step can yield an apology that falls short. For example, without framing the disruptive behavior in the past, there could be misinterpretations of what the apology is all about because people need to put the behavior back in proper perspective. And without acknowledging how the offensive behavior affected someone, this could result in a shallow apology. Further, without sorrow, the offended person may perceive that there is no genuine interest in apologizing. Finally, the rubber meets the road if the person apologizing has no intention in changing her/his behavior. If the

TABLE 1.10

Rationales Associated with Each of the Phases of the Four-Step Apology

1. The concrete action framed in the past: In order to zero in on the offensive action so there is no misinterpretation.
2. How the action affected others: To be certain that your action was perceived as offensive.
3. Sorrow: Because the offended party needs to hear this.
4. Future reparation: In order for the apology to be genuine; repeating the offensive actions will likely negate this authenticity.

person's behavior continues after the apology, this person has lost further ground: the offended individual may avoid the toxic person in the future or worse, he/she may quit. To make this four-step apology as robust as possible, Table 1.10 illustrates some of the rationales within each of the phases.

2

Myths about Toxic Behaviors

There are many misconceptions about toxic behaviors. When these misconceptions are regarded as facts, myths emerge. Some myths are correct, but others are not. Before determining ways to work with toxic people, it is important to understand the myths that operationalize our way of thinking about them—and uncover the truths that debunk these myths. This chapter exposes seven myths that prevent us from working successfully with these uncivil individuals (Table 2.1).

MYTH #1: YOU CAN'T CALCULATE
THE FINANCIAL COST OF TOXIC PEOPLE

While we all recognize the emotional toll that toxic people pass on to others, we are much more reticent in determining the financial cost of their behaviors. While this is not to underestimate the person's impact on our psyches and own well-being, money sometimes sells. What I mean by this is that often individuals are reluctant to "bare their souls" to management about the emotional suffering caused by a toxic person. However, when financial costs are presented, the organization now has a business case for doing something about it. Leaders are more likely to listen.

> Often individuals are reluctant to "bare their souls" to management about the emotional suffering caused by the toxic person. However, when financial costs are presented, the organization now has a business case for doing something about it. Leaders are more likely to listen.

In this section, I bust the myth that it is impossible to determine the costs of toxic behavior. I present the business case through a formula for

TABLE 2.1

Myths about Toxic People

- **Myth #1: You can't calculate the financial cost of toxic people**
  Truth: Not only can you arrive at what toxic people cost organizations financially, you will also be able to use this to sell others on the importance of taking action.
- **Myth #2: Many toxic people are incompetent**
  Truth: Many times they are not; this makes dealing with them even more difficult.
- **Myth #3: Ignoring the toxic person will stop the behavior**
  Truth: Not necessarily.
- **Myth #4: Concrete feedback will handle their manipulations**
  Truth: Only if the feedback is positioned correctly.
- **Myth #5: Making up your mind you won't put up with toxic behaviors is enough**
  Truth: In reality, many put up with them for very long periods of time.
- **Myth #6: There's little you can do if your boss is toxic**
  Truth: Not so fast! There are strategies that can work with bosses.
- **Myth #7: Keeping the problem to yourself will protect you in the long run**
  Truth: Keeping it to yourself may prolong the agony and not allow you to get the help you need.

---

determining the financial costs associated with having to replace employees who quit as a result of a toxic person. Many times, those who quit may be some of your top employees. Hopefully, this formula will convince you to take action, since this documents how toxic people are interfering with your organization's financial success. It will likely help you "sell" the fact that something needs to be done such that toxic people don't get away with bad behavior. Money sometimes talks!

This formula is presented with an interactive spreadsheet and is meant to help you understand the financial impact of these individuals *and* to convince others that dealing with toxic behavior is a key to good business. By going to the following website, www.mitchellkusy.com, you can obtain the interactive spreadsheet on which you can work directly using your own organizational statistics. It is entitled *The Kusy Toxic Cost Worksheet*. To engage this worksheet, you will need two primary statistics to determine the impact of toxic people in your organization:

- *Number of employees* in each of three categories in your organization:
  - Entry-level staff
  - Mid-level professionals and managers
  - High-level executives and highly specialized professionals

- *Average compensation* for each of these three employee categories:
  - Entry-level staff
  - Mid-level professionals and managers
  - High-level executives and highly specialized professionals

If you do not have these exact statistics per category, I suggest you not be overly concerned. Estimations in each category are fine because the purpose is to garner some insights as to the overall financial impact of toxic people. Even with very conservative estimates, I believe you will likely be surprised how much toxic people cost organizations.

Once you enter the data into the spreadsheet, you will see the replacement costs associated with people who quit as a result of a toxic person. Determination of these costs is based on several research studies as indicated in Table 2.2. To interpolate these statistics for application into the interactive spreadsheet, the following assumptions provide a rationale. First, since 64 percent are likely to currently work with a toxic person, 45 percent of which lash out at least two to three times per week (Kusy & Holloway, 2009), this is therefore a serious problem affecting approximately 28 percent of the work population (64% × 45% = 28%). Second, since 12 percent quit as a result of uncivil behavior (Pearson & Porath, 2009), this is 3 percent of the work population (28% × 12% = 3%). Third, depending upon the category of employee compensation (i.e., entry-level, mid-level, or high-level/highly specialized), the cost of turnover to the organization is 3% × salary of 30%, 150%, or 400%, respectively.

Further, here are some explanatory perspectives related to this spreadsheet. I use the term "organization" in a generic sense to mean a social system, which can be the entire organization or a department, division, or team within your organization. This allows you to determine the cost for the entire organization (if this is your context) or for a smaller social system within the organization such as a team, division, or department.

TABLE 2.2

Statistics Associated with Toxic People and Turnover

- **64%** are likely to currently work with a toxic person (Kusy & Holloway, 2009)
- **45%** reported that the toxic person projected their negative behaviors onto others at least two to three times per week (Kusy & Holloway, 2009)
- **12%** quit as a result of uncivil behavior; **92%** reduced effort (Pearson & Porath, 2009)
- **30%, 150%, and 400%** are the replacement costs for employees who quit in each of three categories of employees, respectively: entry-level, mid-level, high-level/highly specialized (Borysenko, 2015)

Second, if the employee categories don't quite fit, that's OK. You want a "ballpark" figure that provides motivation and momentum to do something about this problem. The reason that there are three employee categories is to align with the research on the cost of replacing three categories of individuals. If you have difficulty in using the percentages associated with the three categories, then simply select the category of employee that best applies to your context.

To see how this plays out, I have created three fictitious organizations based upon size—small, medium, and large—and applied the related statistics in Figure 2.1. To use this interactive spreadsheet tool in your organization, please visit my website (www.mitchellkusy.com). Figure 2.1 applies the statistics of number of employees and average compensation to an organization small in size. As indicated in Figure 2.1, step 1 is to indicate the number of employees in each of three categories. Assume that this small organization has 100 employees with 75 entry-level, 20 mid-level, and 5 high-level/highly specialized workers. Enter these data into your interactive spreadsheet. Step 2 is used to indicate the average compensation in

Step 1. Identify the number of employees in your span of influence or the entire organization in one, two, or all three employee categories			
# of entry level	# of mid-level	# of high-level	Total # of employees in your span of influence
75	20	5	100
Estimated number of employees working with an extremely toxic employee			
21.75	5.8	1.45	29
Estimated number of employees who quit as a result of working with a toxic employee			
# of entry level	# of mid-level	# of high-level	Total # of employees who quit
2.61	0.70	0.17	3.48
Step 2. Calculate average annual compensation for employees in the categories identified in Step 1			
Average compensation entry level $25,000.00	Average compensation mid-level $60,000.00	Average compensation high-level $100,000.00	Total average compensation all employees $3,575,000.00
Overall costs of replacing ONE employee who quits at various levels			
Entry level cost $7,500.00	Mid-level cost $90,000.00	High-level cost $400,000.00	Total replacement costs $497,500.00
Replacement costs for employees who quit as a result of working with an extremely toxic employee			
Entry level cost $19,575.00	Mid-level cost $62,640.00	High-level cost $69,600.00	Total replacement costs $151,815.00

FIGURE 2.1
Sample case spreadsheet for determining the replacement costs for people who quit as a result of toxic people in a small organization.

each of these three categories (i.e., $25,000 at the entry-level, $60,000 at the mid-level, and $100,000 at the high-level/highly specialized). The results indicate that the total compensation for all employee groups is $3,575,000. The cost of turnover due to toxic people is $151,815, which is 4 percent of total compensation.

In a medium-size organization you will see the following statistics applied in Figure 2.2. As in the previous example with a small organization, step 1 serves to indicate the number of employees in each of three categories. Assume that this medium-size organization has 2000 employees among which are 1500 entry-level, 475 mid-level, and 25 high-level/highly specialized workers. Enter these data into your interactive spreadsheet. In step 2 define the average compensation in each of these three categories (i.e. $30,000 at the entry-level, $70,000 at the mid-level, and $125,000 at the high-level/highly specialized). The results indicate that the total compensation for all employee groups is $81,375,000. The cost of turnover due to toxic people is $2,640,250, which is 3 percent of total compensation.

Step 1. Identify the number of employees in your span of influence or the entire organization in one, two, or all three employee categories			
# of entry level 1500	# of mid-level 475	# of high-level 25	Total # of employees in your span of influence 2000
Estimated number of employees working with an extremely toxic employee			
435	137.75	7.25	580
Estimated number of employees who quit as a result of working with a toxic employee			
# of entry level 52.20	# of mid-level 16.53	# of high-level 0.87	Total # of employees who quit 69.60
Step 2. Calculate average annual compensation for employees in the categories identified in Step 1			
Average compensation entry level $30,000.00	Average compensation mid-level $70,000.00	Average compensation high-level $125,000.00	Total average compensation all employees $81,375,000.00
Overall costs of replacing ONE employee who quits at various levels			
Entry level cost $9,000.00	Mid-level cost $105,000.00	High-level cost $500,000.00	Total replacement costs $614,000.00
Replacement costs for employees who quit as a result of working with an extremely toxic employee			
Entry level cost $469,800.00	Mid-level cost $1,735,650.00	High-level cost $435,000.00	Total replacement costs $2,640,450.00

FIGURE 2.2
Sample case template for determining the replacement costs for people who quit as a result of toxic people in a medium-size organization.

In a large organization, Figure 2.3 illustrates a similar set of statistics. Assume that this large organization has 20,000 employees with 15,000 entry-level, 4700 mid-level, and 300 high-level/highly specialized jobs. Enter these data into your interactive spreadsheet. In step 2 again, define the average compensation in each of these three categories (i.e., $30,000 at the entry-level, $65,000 at the mid-level, and $150,000 at the high-level/highly specialized). The results indicate that the total compensation for all employee groups is $800,500,000. The cost of turnover due to toxic people is $26,909,100, again 3 pecent of total compensation.

In all three scenarios of small, medium, and large organizations, applying the formula using number of employees and average compensation will reveal the financial cost of toxic people. This cost in these examples can range from 3 to 4 percent of payroll costs! Hopefully, you will see that I was quite conservative in my compensation amounts. If the compensation

Step 1. Identify the number of employees in your span of influence or the entire organization in one, two, or all three employee categories			
# of entry level 15,000	# of mid-level 4700	# of high-level 300	Total # of employees in your span of influence 20,000
Estimated number of employees working with an extremely toxic employee			
4350	1363	87	5800
Estimated number of employees who quit as a result of working with a toxic employee			
# of entry level 522.00	# of mid-level 163.56	# of high-level 10.44	Total # of employees who quit 696.00
Step 2. Calculate average annual compensation for employees in the categories identified in Step 1			
Average compensation entry level $30,000.00	Average compensation mid-level $65,000.00	Average compensation high-level $150,000.00	Total average compensation all employees $800,500,000.00
Overall costs of replacing ONE employee who quits at various levels			
Entry level cost $9,000.00	Mid-level cost $97,500.00	High-level cost $600,000.00	Total replacement costs $706,500.00
Replacement costs for employees who quit as a result of working with an extremely toxic employee			
Entry level cost $4,698,000.00	Mid-level cost $15,947,100.00	High-level cost $6,264,000.00	Total replacement costs $26,909,100.00

FIGURE 2.3
Sample case template for determining the replacement costs for people who quit as a result of toxic people in a large organization.

is higher in your organization than in my examples, you will experience more financial losses by not doing something about toxic people in your organization. Your own results may vary based on your organization's actual labor costs and the mix of employees in each of the categories there. And these are just the replacement costs for employees who quit. Other research has found that 22 percent of targets of incivility reduced their work effort and time spent at work (Pearson & Porath, 2009). My own organizational clients, who often seek ways to be more effective and efficient, have shared with me that this kind of cost savings is of a kind they had never anticipated. Now they can by employing this formula.

> In all three scenarios of small, medium, and large organizations, applying the formula using number of employees and average compensation will reveal the financial cost of toxic people. This cost in these examples ranged from 3 to 4 percent of payroll costs!

In addition to this generic template for all industries, there are compelling statistics that can be applied for those who work in the healthcare sector. These statistics come from several studies authored by some of the most renowned healthcare researchers (Rosenstein, 2010; Rosenstein & O'Daniel, 2005, 2008) and can help make the case that patient safety and service are at stake. For example, in the general population, 64 percent currently experience toxic behaviors; in healthcare it is 80 percent. Another clear and relevant example is the impact on patient safety—a benchmark in healthcare. So, if 50 percent of those who witnessed toxic, disruptive behaviors believed that it affected patient safety, this is a standalone statistic that must be acknowledged. Even more compelling is the fact that 25 percent of those who witnessed this behavior associated it with patient death. Hopefully, even those who do not work in healthcare may want to be more mindful of these disruptive actions because these can affect your own safety as a patient. Personally, it is on my mind when I have a medical appointment with my provider!

Additional healthcare statistics from the National Healthcare Retention & RN Staffing Report include the fact that the direct costs of RN nurse turnover can be between $37,700 to $58,400 (NSI Nursing Solutions Inc., 2016). Add to this their annual salary and you can quickly assess the financial impact. The research previously cited in the general population found that for mid-level professionals, the replacement costs are 150 percent of annual salary while for highly specialized employees, this can be as high as 400 percent. So,

TABLE 2.3

Summary Statistics of the Impact of Disruptive Behaviors on the Nursing Profession from the 2016 National Healthcare Retention & RN Staffing Report

---

- **70%:** The percentage of nurses who saw an association between disruptive behaviors and compromises in quality of patient care
- **$2,000 to $5,800:** The amount an adverse drug has per hospitalization
- **2.2 to 4.6 days:** The increased hospitalization as a result of adverse drug impact

---

depending upon the level and training of the nurse, there's a spread of 150 to 400 percent of annual salary for replacement costs.

More than 70 percent of RNs in the 2016 National Healthcare Retention & RN Staffing Report saw the direct link between toxic behaviors and compromises in quality of patient care and the occurrence of medical errors. The cost of an adverse drug event ranges from $2,000 to $5,800 per hospitalization and an increased length of stay from 2.2 to 4.6 days. So, it may be important to consider these data for those who work in healthcare. It's not just about the bottom line. It's about life. It's about length of hospital stay. It's about risk of infections. When people working in healthcare teams are not communicating with each other in order to avoid confrontation, ridicule, and shaming—there is real human cost. Table 2.3 provides you with a summary of these statistics from the 2016 National Healthcare Retention & RN Staffing Report (NSI Nursing Solutions Inc., 2016).

MYTH #2: MANY TOXIC PEOPLE ARE INCOMPETENT

Surprisingly, many toxic people are highly competent and bring a special expertise to their organizations. This creates a precarious situation about which many leaders lament, echoed by the following sentiment: "If I give them negative feedback, what if they quit?" But by not giving them feedback, you are setting yourself up for a vicious cycle even if they stay. For example, if you have tried giving feedback several times, stating the consequences of what will happen if the behavior does not stop, but have not followed through on these stated consequences, the person may interpret from your behavior that you do not stand behind your word. Consequently, the toxic behavior continues. Does this mean that you cannot give them feedback? Certainly not. However, the feedback needs to take into consideration an understanding of the systemic effects of the toxic person's behavior, being able to share these with her/him, and sticking to a stated course of action. This process will be explored in great detail in Chapter 3, where I will explore specific strategies.

> Surprisingly, many toxic people are highly competent and bring a special expertise to their organizations. This creates a precarious situation about which many leaders lament, echoed by the following sentiment: "If I give them negative feedback, what if they quit?" But by not giving them feedback, you are setting yourself up for a vicious cycle even if they stay.

While working with thousands of leaders for over 35 years, I have discovered that while many toxic people threaten to quit, very few actually do. And for those who do quit, count your blessings! And while losing these talents can be difficult to navigate, please remember the statistics presented in Table 2.2. Specifically, the trauma created by these uncivil individuals causes others to quit (12% of targets of their venom quit), costs the organization money to replace these individuals (with costs ranging from 30% to 400% of the person's compensation), and results in reduced work effort and time spent at work (22% lost productivity). One of the most effective strategies in these circumstances with highly competent people is to remember the hard data: doing nothing costs your organization money. And if you are in healthcare, add reduced patient safety to the list!

Further, consider those who are targets of the toxic person's behavior; many of these targets are highly competent. Toxic behavior drives these highly competent targeted professionals away from your organization.

> Consider those who are targets of the toxic person's behavior; many of these targets are highly competent. Toxic behavior drives these highly competent targeted professionals away from your organization.

MYTH #3: IGNORING THE TOXIC PERSON WILL STOP THE BEHAVIOR

This myth is a paradox. On one end of the spectrum, reinforcement theory tells us that when we stop reinforcing the behavior, the behavior extinguishes. On the other end, this is often what does *not* happen with toxic people. Why? In my own consulting practice I have discovered that they have an incredibly long fuse. Essentially, their behavior lasts long enough to push many of us past our threshold. Part of this may have to do with their self-centered nature. As such, when they hear things about their behaviors, there's a strong tendency to turn this around—that it's about someone else. Therefore, they feel there's no rationale for them to stop. Another reason may have to do with the fact that when their negative behaviors are ignored, they may find other targets. As you may have experienced, their behaviors are quite transferable to others!

So, then what happens? It's a spiral downward of increasingly maladaptive behaviors. Consider Figure 2.4 that describes a case that a client recently related to me.

While certainly not all scenarios have this spiraling downward slope, many do. Leaders cannot ignore these behaviors when brought to their attention. Remember what was reported in Chapter 1: many of these individuals are chameleons, capable of "knocking down and kissing up." When these behaviors are brought to your attention, you need to investigate and not assume it's just "someone's way." Attributing it to one's personality is essentially ignoring the situation.

> Many of these individuals are chameleons, capable of "knocking down and kissing up." When these behaviors are brought to your attention, you need to investigate and not assume it's just "someone's way." Attributing it to one's personality is essentially ignoring the situation.

Person criticizes the target person mercilessly in private.

Target person ignores. Person continues with the private attacks and expands into settings where she now has an audience.

Toxic person continues the attacks. Others intervene and say something to the toxic individual to quell her behavior.

The toxic person confronts target person and asks why he talked about her to others.

Target person goes to boss, who says that it's just her "personality" and to let it fly off your back.

Target person decides it's not worth it. Interviews for other jobs. Finds one. Quits.

FIGURE 2.4

The downward spiral of ignoring a toxic person.

MYTH #4: CONCRETE FEEDBACK WILL HANDLE THEIR MANIPULATIONS

There are several dimensions of feedback that make this myth a tricky one. Table 2.4 describes the three primary syndromes I have discovered that make giving feedback so difficult.

The first is a "holier-than-thou" attitude that applies to a recent scenario described by a client of mine. My client gave some very concrete, non-evaluative feedback to her toxic direct report, who responded in the following manner: "You don't seem to understand. I'm the only one who has the guts to say something about our recent marketing campaign. I'm the only one who will let our marketing VP have it. If it weren't for me, this company would be in a shambles." I think you get the picture here. Without this toxic person the place would fall apart was the logic. This is how many toxic people respond to receiving feedback about their behavior when they also believe themselves to be essential. In this situation, you don't want to get into a battle with the toxic person because many are very good at sharing how they are better than others—their answer to why you're wrong. Instead, you want to take the wind out of their sails. Simply saying the following will do: "I'm not going to get into a battle over this. I'm sharing with you regarding the impact this has on me, and possibly others."

The second maneuver regarding their "nearsightedness" stems from the fact that the person does not have a long-term gauge in how they see their behavior. Specifically, they may not see the impact of their behavior on others. One of my colleagues, who is a leadership coach, shared the following case with me. A person she was recently coaching reported how his behaviors were actually helping build the team. When the coach asked how this could be, the person responded that he's got the best-performing team in the company. Probing further, the coach asked about the turnover

TABLE 2.4

Three Maneuvers That Make Giving Uncivil People Feedback So Perplexing

- *Holier than thou:* They turn your feedback around in such a way that they may acknowledge they do this, *but* do so for the right reasons
- *Nearsightedness:* They may acknowledge the behavior but not the impact of their behavior on others over the long term
- *Bait-and-switch tactic:* They shift gears by saying this is your problem and no one else has these kinds of problems with him/her

on the team. The person proudly stated that it's 50 percent because he only wants the best. While it is difficult to determine if the 50 percent who left were all poor performers, it is unlikely based on the research already carried out by many—the best performers have a tendency to quit when they work with a toxic person. This individual could not even fathom that he might be part of the problem! So, sharing a relevant statistic regarding such things as turnover may at least help the person pause, reflect, and then act. Some uncivil individuals understand what they are doing in the present tense but do not understand the long-term consequences of their behaviors. If you will recall our study (Kusy & Holloway, 2009), 51 percent of the targets of the incivility stated that they would likely look for another job. And that is exactly what happened in this case.

The third behavioral maneuver is one that presents a reversal, in which the person asserts "*You* have the problem." This is a clever tactic that is often based on the fact that others don't seem to have problems with this person. The toxic person may even argue that if you had more of anything (e.g., sensitivity, guts, values, etc.), you would see that this is clearly your problem, not the toxic person's. This is a "bait-and-switch" maneuver that deflects from the real issue. How to respond? Something like the following: "I do not agree that this is my problem. However, I would like to make two suggestions. First, please take some time to reflect a bit on what I have said and consider if there is at least some validity in it. Perhaps, go through some scenarios of past team meetings in which you engaged in this behavior. Second, you may want to ask others whom you respect and know you well about this."

All three maneuvers are manipulative, intended to allow the person to continue their behavior unabashedly. Table 2.5 summarizes why these strategies are manipulative.

TABLE 2.5

Why Uncivil People's Maneuvers to Defend Themselves Are Manipulative

- *Holier than thou:* The toxic person's condescension can put the target on the defensive and be less apt to work through the problem
- *Nearsightedness:* Not seeing the long-term effects of their behaviors can result in their thinking that it is not that big a deal; thus they believe it is OK to continue these behaviors
- *Bait-and-switch tactic:* By making this *your* problem, they attempt to deflect the focus from their own uncivil behavior

MYTH #5: MAKING UP YOUR MIND YOU WON'T PUT UP WITH TOXIC BEHAVIORS IS ENOUGH

It's not very difficult to understand how toxic people get under our skin. The examples described thus far are likely aligned with some of your experiences. While it is easy to say we will not put up with them, the unfortunate reality is that many of us do. As testified by one respondent in our research study, we found that these behaviors could go on for upwards of 30 years (Kusy & Holloway, 2009). There are four factors contributing to the longevity of these behaviors, as identified in Table 2.6.

The first of these is a simple one—there is a perception that feedback doesn't seem to work. Why? The system supports the toxic behaviors. How? Because there is a perception that giving feedback (and bearing the consequences of this) is more painful than simply going along with the person. I say "perception" because you have already discovered the long-term effects of these people, and know that the consequences of letting them be is far more detrimental to a company. In addition, many don't know how to give effective feedback that can make a difference. You will discover in Chapter 3 that there are ways to give feedback that *will* improve the probability of success.

Another reason people put up with toxic behaviors for a long time is something I refer to as "secondary gain." Here's a real example from a recent experience I had with someone working with a toxic person. I asked what happened to the team when the person was not around, and I was

TABLE 2.6

Why Organizations Put Up with Toxic People for Many Years

1. Perception that giving feedback is:
   - More painful than bearing the consequences
   - Difficult because some don't know how to do it effectively
2. "Secondary gain" becomes a modus operandi because:
   - Some get gratification out of talking about the situation
   - Others prefer to wallow in the "ain't-it-awful" syndrome
3. Excuses of toxic people can be rampant and just; what if…
   - The excuses make sense?
   - They call you on your behavior and you're put on the defensive?
4. Fear of the unknown continues the status quo because:
   - What if the replacement person is worse?
   - What if we can't find a replacement?

told that they talk about how disastrous these behaviors are for the team. Upon further probing, I asked this person to describe this for me in concrete ways. Here's what they shared with each other:

- "It's awful to see how Jim is treating his boss."
- "He runs over her like a steamroller."
- "Just last week he told everyone at our team meeting that we are running this department into the ground."

Do you sense what is happening here? It's gossip. And people get a lot of "secondary gain" out of gossiping. Gossip can cement the team in a cohesive (albeit negative) way, by pitting everyone against the toxic person. The reason I say this cohesion is negative is based on what I have discovered happens afterwards. When the person departs from the organization (either is fired or leaves on his own), teams that thrive on "secondary gain" often do not know how to relate positively to each other; they have built the team on gossiping about the person!

> When the toxic person departs the organization (either is fired or leaves on his own), teams that thrive on "secondary gain" often do not know how to relate positively to each other; they have built the team on gossiping about the person!

The third reason others put up with toxic people is that their excuses run rampant. In the beginning, these excuses may almost make sense, but as time goes on, people start to become wary. However, if you are the manager of this individual and have allowed it to go on for so long, it may now be difficult to tackle the toxic person with direct feedback. If you do, you may find the toxic individual calling you out on this, wondering why you have not said anything before. And you know what, they're right! But just because they are right is no excuse for you not to do something! The best time to start is now. If you are in this situation, feel free to jump ahead to Chapter 3 that focuses on how to give the best possible feedback that works. In addition, here's a tip for those who have ignored giving feedback. Start with something like: "While I know I have not been effective in talking with you about your behavior that has negatively impacted the team, I'm going to start now. Rather than go back in time, I want to share two observations with you that occurred over the past week." With this type of opening strategy where you acknowledge your failure and do not bring up historical behaviors, you are likely to take the wind out of their sails. It is honest, straightforward, and works quite effectively.

> Here's a tip for those who have ignored giving feedback. Start with something like: "While I know I have not been effective in talking with you about your behavior that has negatively impacted the team, I'm going to start now. Rather than go back in time, I want to share two observations with you that occurred over the past week."

Finally, fear of the unknown further allows these behaviors to continue for a long time. Some of the fears that leaders have involve concerns about finding a suitable replacement, not being able to afford a replacement, and facing a possible lawsuit should you fire the toxic person. Before operating on these fears, the pro–con assessment I have identified in Chapter 3 will help you discern whether you want to take action at all.

MYTH #6: THERE'S LITTLE YOU CAN DO IF YOUR BOSS IS TOXIC

Of all the issues that come up with my clients, this one is often at the top of the list. What if I have a boss who is a toxic person? The good news here is that you do not need to throw in the towel. There is hope! There are two primary strategies that increase the probability of successfully dealing with a toxic boss that I address in great detail in Chapter 3:

- Assess whether or not it's in your best interest to give feedback to your toxic boss;
- And, if it is in your best interest, structure this feedback in a coherent and concrete way.

Chapter 3 addresses the challenges of working with a toxic boss and what to do about it. What is important to remember is that a toxic boss does not need to degrade you, your worth, or your pride. With the two strategies proposed in Chapter 3—the cost-benefit strategy and the boss strategy—you will improve your chances of dealing with a toxic boss.

The cost-benefit strategy deals with how to accurately assess whether you even *want* to entertain having a conversation with your boss. You will assess the perils of remaining in your current position with the status quo, remaining in your position with feedback, or leaving. Then, you can make an informed decision.

If you decide to stay, then the boss strategy focuses on *how* to have a conversation with your toxic boss. It outlines a progression of the conversation with clear markers along the way. If productive, you will have a more successful experience with your boss. If not, you can revert to the cost-benefit strategy for a determination regarding the best next step for you.

MYTH #7: KEEPING THE PROBLEM TO YOURSELF WILL PROTECT YOU IN THE LONG RUN

We have just discussed the negative ramifications of gossiping, but this does not mean keeping toxic situations to yourself. Instead, a mentor is vital to giving you a healthy way of dealing with the toxic person. I use the term "healthy" to refer to both emotional and physical health. While the emotional effects of a toxic person are evident in such feelings as a sense of worthlessness, loss of pride, lack of respect in one's own work, and humiliation, the physical effects are not as evident. Physical responses to these kinds of behaviors can increase our blood pressure, blood glucose, and cholesterol levels, as well as decrease the body's immune system (Klein & Forni, 2011).

I have found that a mentor who is insightful about organizational politics and adept at understanding organizational challenges—such as toxic individuals—is a vital link to helping you deal with these behaviors. One mentor with whom I recently chatted helped her mentee understand the power of staying clear of the gossip fray. In addition, she supported the target of incivility by helping him understand ways to give *positive* feedback to the toxic person when the person actually acted like a human being!

Another benefit of working with a mentor is that this person is a good barometer to gauge the accuracy of what you may be telling yourself. Table 2.7 identifies some of the inaccurate ideas and assumptions I have heard over the years—all of which prevent taking the first step toward positive action. In this inventory, please check how likely it is you have made these statements related to a toxic person with whom you have interacted. Then, with a mentor or trusted friend/colleague, share this with them.

TABLE 2.7

Inventory of Inaccurate Ideas and Assumptions That Targets of Toxic Behaviors Often Have

Instructions: As you think about a specific toxic person with whom you are having difficulty, determine if any of the statements below represent some of your thinking. Rate how likely or unlikely these statements reflect your thinking. Then, share the results with a mentor or trusted colleague/friend. Discuss those that impact you the most. Before taking action, I suggest you read the remainder of the book because this will help you target your potential action strategy.

	Likely to Think This:	Unlikely to Think This:
1. "I'll alter my schedule a bit and then will have less interaction with the toxic person."	O	O
2. "It's just a matter of time, and someone else will catch this person in the act."	O	O
3. "I'll be better off if I just mind my own business"	O	O
4. "I will just punch in my hours like a time clock, and not offer to work any extra hours."	O	O
5. "If I confront this person, I will be worse off."	O	O
6. "I've tried to intervene with this person. It failed. I'd better leave well enough alone."	O	O
7. "I could never go to this person's boss about this. That would be political suicide."	O	O
8. "It must be about me. If I accommodated this person more, I might have better luck."	O	O

Listen. And then have a conversation about this and determine which are inaccurate and what you might want to do about it.

In addition, a strategy that could work for anyone who does have a mentor is to discuss various strategies identified in this book, and see what might work with the uncivil individual. When discussing these various strategies, I suggest assessing the pros and cons, then selecting the one that is the best fit for your needs.

I have also seen mentors help individuals understand the power of getting away from day-to-day work activities. For example, one mentor suggested how important physical exercise can be in simply letting go. While this does *not* mean ignoring the situation, it does mean that sometimes the benefits of exercise may help us become more relaxed and able to deal with the situation much more proactively. Another mentor helped someone get away from the system by actually taking them away from work on

TABLE 2.8

How Mentors Can Support Individuals Who Are Targets of Incivility

- Help individuals who are targets of incivility see their worth
- Support these individuals in understanding the importance of getting away at times from the system that plagues them
- Help in brainstorming for new ways of thinking about a situation
- Help individuals generate new ways of resolving a situation
- Provide creative ways to cope

a regular basis—as a volunteer in a soup kitchen for homeless individuals. These "getting away" activities helped the affected individual get a better sense of perspective. The result was that she dealt with the toxic person head-on, but in a respectful way by giving feedback on just one behavior that was most important to her. Previously, she said she would have come up with "dozens" of aversive behaviors from this person that just rubbed her the wrong way. Now, she just seemed more focused in addressing the behavior that was most in need of correction. She attributed the success of this venture first to her mentor who helped her find this alternative activity; second, to the experience in the soup kitchen. No easy answers here. But a well-selected mentor is powerful in effective brainstorming and problem solving. Table 2.8 describes how some mentors have supported individuals who are targets of incivility.

As you can see from Table 2.8, a good mentor is likely not the answer to the problem, but more the generator of potential options that the targeted individual may not have considered. It certainly does "take a village." The interesting discovery here is that too often, we attempt to do it alone. When we engage others in supporting our efforts to do something about this kind of problem, there are greater opportunities for positive outcomes.

3

Powerful Ways to Give Toxic People Feedback

"Why am I wasting time giving feedback to an uncivil person? It doesn't work and I just get myself into further hot water." This lament from one of my recent clients demonstrates the frustration felt when feedback backfires. There has been a reluctance to have a conversation with a toxic person because of the tremendous intimidation factor that often comes with working with them. More poignantly, there has been a reluctance to give the toxic person feedback. But there are many support systems that should be in place to increase the success of this type of conversation—as identified in each of the chapters. However, even if you are not able to implement any of these systemic approaches, this chapter will help you determine how to best position the conversation *and* make it successful.

The bad news first. As stated in Chapter 1, many toxic people are clueless regarding the full-blown impact of their behaviors. Does this mean feedback does not work? Certainly not. But, diplomacy and a structured process are needed. The art of diplomacy needs to be partnered with direct, firm, precise delivery in order to gain the maximum opportunity for results.

To this end, I offer a menu of four strategies that will help you be as efficient and effective as possible in providing feedback to the uncivil individual (Table 3.1). The first strategy—the cost-benefit strategy—is a must. Then, depending upon the results of this strategy, the remaining three strategies will play out according to your needs.

TABLE 3.1

Four Types of Feedback Strategies

- *Cost-benefit strategy* to determine whether or not you should initiate a feedback conversation with the person about his/her behavior
- *Direct report strategy* to explain to the toxic person who reports to you the significance of her/his behavior to others
- *Peer strategy* to provide feedback to a peer when there is no direct reporting relationship
- *Boss strategy* to give feedback to your toxic boss and help him/her understand the impact of the boss's behavior on others

---

COST-BENEFIT STRATEGY

One of the most difficult decisions a leader has to make regarding uncivil people is whether to give them feedback. There are many intervening variables at play here. I have designed the cost-benefit strategy to take into consideration these important factors, which take some of the guesswork out of this process. With the careful weighing of these factors, you will make a more informed and effective decision. Table 3.2 identifies the five core components of a cost-benefit analysis for assessing whether or not to have a conversation with this individual.

The very first thing to do is weigh the pros and cons of whether or not you should give feedback. To help you do this, please consider responding to the questions in the pro-con analysis (Table 3.3).

After weighing the pros and cons, your next call to action is to check out your evaluation with someone you trust. The trusted individual may be a peer, a coach, or someone in your Employee Assistance Program (EAP), if your organization has one. Take the time to do this and really listen to

TABLE 3.2

Cost-Benefit Strategy to Determine the Worth
of a Conversation with a Toxic Individual

Weigh the pros and cons of providing feedback.
Overview the pros and cons with someone you trust.
Reduce these to one of three options:
- Remain in your position and give feedback.
- Remain in your position and do not give feedback.
- Leave your position.

Take a day or so before acting on the final option.
Heal. Move on.

TABLE 3.3

Pro-Con Analysis Inventory

Color in the circle corresponding with the response that most closely approximates your perspective. When you analyze your responses, the more items toward the "highly likely" end of the scale will indicate that you should pause and be concerned about giving feedback. This does *not* mean that you should not give feedback. Just pause and reflect.

	Not Likely	Somewhat Likely	Highly Likely	Not Applicable
1. Has feedback to the toxic person from others been largely ineffective?	O	O	O	O
2. Has feedback from others backfired such that they have simply given up?	O	O	O	O
3. Are there serious consequences that can occur precluding me from giving feedback?	O	O	O	O
4. To what extent am I trying to prove (with feedback) that I am right?	O	O	O	O
5. Is the feedback a retaliatory move on my part?	O	O	O	O
6. Has someone I trust warned me not to give feedback?	O	O	O	O

the response. Then, take a day or so to make your final decision using any one of these three approaches: stay and give feedback, stay and do not give feedback, or leave.

Regarding the third option of leaving, this does not necessarily mean leaving the organization. There may be opportunities to apply for another position within the organization. Think carefully on whether your problem is with your specific situation, or with the organization as a whole.

Finally, and quite importantly—whatever you decide—take some time to heal. It is likely that you have been seriously affected by this person's behavior and need to be gentle on yourself. Beyond this gentleness, part of the healing is to move on. You could be ready to move on right away, but if not, you may need to talk with someone about this. Perhaps your trusted colleague? Your organization's Employee Assistance Program (EAP)? A spouse? Friend? Significant other? A counselor?

If you have made the decision to proceed with the conversation, timing is crucial. Consider the best times to approach the individual, as well as the worst times. In general, the best times are those when the person is engaged in the least amount of frenetic energy—when not busy. Do not corner the individual in a public space; find a quiet time to ask when

TABLE 3.4

Times When Best to Give Feedback to a Toxic Individual

- During times when the individual is least busy
- When the individual is not in a public space
- When there is a quiet space available
- Usually not if the individual is multitasking, in an attempt to just get the feedback "done with"

would be a good time for a conversation about something important to your working relationship. The individual may say "now," so be prepared to have this conversation. And if the person says when they might have time (even now), be prepared to give them an estimate of how much time this will take. I suggest 30 minutes as a good starting point. Consider this strategy of finding the best time to proceed with the conversation—whether it's with your direct report, peer, or boss. In Table 3.4, you will see some considerations for how best to time giving feedback to a toxic individual.

DIRECT REPORT STRATEGY

If you are the boss working with a direct report, the good news is that influence is on your side. But it is important not to be cavalier about it. Many bosses struggle with this for a variety of reasons. Table 3.5 identifies some of the top reasons that bosses are reluctant to give feedback to a direct report.

Whatever the reason, what *is* important is that the longer you wait to give feedback to a toxic direct report, the more difficult the challenge becomes. It snowballs. Hopefully, the direct report strategy will provide

TABLE 3.5

Examples of the Top Reasons Bosses Are Reluctant to Provide Feedback to a Direct Report Who Demonstrates Toxic Behaviors

- "Her performance will slide downward after the feedback."
- "It will be difficult to work with this person once I give feedback."
- "She will tell others that I am a lousy boss."
- "He has a lot of influence in this organization—there goes my good name!"
- "Everyone will know that my team is not as good as I have made it out to be."

TABLE 3.6

The Direct Report Strategy

Describe the behavior and, as appropriate, empathize
Identify the impact of this behavior on others and/or the organization
Request that the individual reflect and respond
Explore alternatives
Choose the best alternative(s)
Tie in a follow-up strategy with your agreement

---

the kind of support a boss needs to put a stake in the ground to do something now. To offset any top-down approach that could negatively impact the results, I have created a template to help you reflect on the conversation you are about to have. Table 3.6 highlights the critical components of this conversation.

> Whatever the reason, what *is* important is that the longer you wait to give feedback to a toxic direct report, the more difficult the challenge becomes. It snowballs. Hopefully, the direct report strategy will provide the kind of support a boss needs to put a stake in the ground to do something now.

As an example, here's a fictitious case scenario that I have built from several client situations over the years:

Describe behavior:

> *Boss:* "Dave, I want to talk with you about what I have been observing in our team meetings. Specifically, you have been interrupting others to the point that people are asking me what is going on. Related to the interrupting, you have also come down on others pretty hard. For example, in the meeting last week you told Brenda that anyone who would come up with an idea like hers must not know very much about marketing. I do want you to know that I understand that you have been under a lot of pressure with the recent merger. Unfortunately, that is not an excuse for this kind of behavior."

Identify impact:

> *Boss:* "The impact of this is that the team no longer wants to work with you on our most recent project. I'd like to hear your thoughts, Dave."

Require response:

> *Direct Report:* "I don't agree with you, Sarah. Some of the team members just don't get it. They waste my time with needless chatter about superfluous events and processes. I'm the only one producing this quality and amount of work. I just don't see that there is any need to change my behavior."

Explore alternatives:

> *Boss:* "I don't like hearing this, Dave. Unfortunately, you will need to change your behavior because it is impacting the team's success on this project. I want to work with you on exploring alternatives."

> *Direct Report:* "What kind of alternatives?"

> *Boss:* "Glad you asked that question, Dave. Before I respond, I'd like to hear from you as to what you think you might do?"

> *Direct Report:* "I can't think of anything."

> *Boss:* "OK. I'll start then. What I've been thinking about are four potential strategies. First, I want you to allow people to finish their sentences. You will need to take responsibility for monitoring this and act accordingly. However, if you do not and the behavior continues, I will say something to you like, 'Dave, please don't interrupt. Allow Craig to finish his sentence.' Second, if I see that others are trying to say something and you have spoken a lot more than others who wish to speak, I will cue you with something like, 'Before going on, Dave, I'd like to hear from Linda who has been trying to say something for quite a while.' Third, I will not allow any comments that may be perceived as condescending. Rather than my taking this on, I will throw this to the team. I will ask something like, 'How do others feel about what Dave just said?' If no one responds, I will. Fourth, I am open to first talking with you one-on-one regarding your condescending comments and trying this for a couple of weeks. If this does not resolve the issue, I will bring it up with the team. I know this sounds harsh, Dave, but I simply cannot have this kind of behavior continue because it is eroding our team efforts."

Choose the best alternative(s):

> *Boss:* "Dave, what do you think?"

> *Direct Report:* "Quite frankly, I don't like any of these options. I can't agree to any of these."

> *Boss:* "You will need to or I will choose one or two for you."
> *Direct Report:* "Since you put it that way, I would go with the final option which is talking with me privately about my remarks."

Tie in your agreement with a follow-up strategy:

> *Boss:* "Let's agree to this, then. I will speak with you one-on-one regarding your condescending remarks. I would like to meet with you every Friday to give you feedback—positive or negative. If, after three weeks, your behavior does not change, we will need to revisit this plan; I will then continue with some of the other three options I have just identified. I want you to know that I like that you have selected one option—an option that I believe will work. Let's try this out for three weeks. Agreed?"
> *Direct Report:* "Agreed. But I don't like it."
> *Boss:* "I know that, Dave. I appreciate your working on this plan that I think will create not only a stronger team but also allow you to excel in your own work with the team."

As you can see from this sample case, there is a combination of the boss being firm along with providing some flexibility. Research on changing human behavior demonstrates that people support what they help create. Thus, engagement of others is key. The greater the engagement, the greater the commitment and more successful the follow-through. However, you also need to be structured in setting up a firm plan of action.

One of the most difficult parts of this conversation occurs when the person has an outstanding performance record. However, the leader needs to remember "It takes a village." One high producer does not make a great team. I recall a CEO who told a person on his medical team the following: "You are putting our practice at risk. With the patient complaints we are receiving about you, it does not matter that you have been our highest producer. Patients are now calling in and wanting to transfer to another physician. Our other physicians cannot support this volume so we are having these patients go elsewhere. In addition, because you have not been spending the needed time with each patient and rushing through, you have made some documented errors. This puts our practice at further risk for malpractice insurance claims."

Here you are building a case for your feedback to the toxic person, Another vehicle is to integrate some of the data that I have described earlier. For example, one of my clients positioned the data into the conversation in the following manner: "Tom, we know from research evidence that these behaviors create follow-up actions on the part of others—actions that can be detrimental to our organization. You may not be aware of this, but 51 percent of the targets of these kinds of behaviors consider quitting the organization. And some of those who quit are the organization's top talent. I don't want us to be part of these dismal statistics. Therefore, I'd like to chat with you to help you gain some traction here."

PEER STRATEGY

This is one of the trickiest conversations to have, because you do not have the influence of a boss talking to a direct report. Treading lightly but firmly is the key here. As with bosses, many peers avoid giving feedback to another peer. They give themselves many messages that are founded more on fear than truth. Table 3.7 delineates some of the top reasons a peer may be reluctant to give feedback to another peer.

> Giving feedback to a peer is one of the trickiest conversations to have, because you do not have the influence of a boss talking to a direct report. Treading lightly but firmly is the key here.

While some of the reasons certainly could be true, then a good option is to share your thoughts with a trusted colleague. Ask for their support in guiding you in terms of whether or not you are off base. And hopefully, the previously discussed cost-benefit strategy will help you discern whether you even want to enter into a conversation with your peer. If so, read on. Table 3.8 illustrates the details of the peer strategy.

TABLE 3.7

Examples of the Top Reasons a Peer Is Reluctant to Provide Feedback to Another Peer Demonstrating Toxic Behaviors

---

- "I'm not his boss; that's his boss's job."
- "She wields a lot of power in this school. My name will be mud after this."
- "Maybe I'm just overreacting. Perhaps it's not as bad as I thought."
- "None of my other peers seems to have this problem. Could I be part of the problem?"

TABLE 3.8

Peer Strategy

Position the fact that this is a difficult conversation for you.
Explain the impact of the person's behavior on you and how you have tried to resolve it.
Express that you would like to hear her thoughts.
Review their views and yours.
Set a course of action and a time to follow up.

Here's a sample conversation that should help you understand the style and tenor of the conversation:

Position the conversation:

> *You:* "Sally, I want to start this conversation by saying that it's a difficult one for me. We have always worked well together, except for the last three months, which have been very tough in working with you. Before I ask for your thoughts, let me explain in more detail."

Explain the impact:

> *You:* "Specifically, when you say things to me in front of others like, 'Tom, I would never have made a mistake like that' or 'If you can't agree with me that must mean you are not a team player,' or 'Everyone knows you have a problem with voicing your concern in front of others,' these make me feel like I shouldn't be contributing to the team. Even more, I have made excuses for not attending your project meetings. I have tried to resolve this by stopping you a couple times in the hallway and once in the cafeteria to ask you if you are having any problems with working with me, and you said 'no.'"

Express that you would like to hear their thoughts:

> *You:* "I've talked long enough. I welcome your thoughts."
>
> *Peer:* "Wow! You've really put a lot on me. I don't know how to respond. This is like a real attack on me. I don't know where you get off giving me this kind of feedback. You're not my boss! I can't wait to tell my boss what you just told me. And *your* boss! I simply cannot believe we are having this conversation."

Review their views and yours:

> *You:* "I'm disappointed you feel this way. We disagree. I am not sure how to proceed, but I will try."

Set a course of action and a time to follow up:

> *You:* "While I don't like the fact that we disagree, at least it's now out on the table. I was hoping we could work this out among ourselves. It might be a good idea to have a conversation with our bosses. I would also like to be included. It would be most productive if we can do this together."
>
> *Peer:* "You really know how to ruin someone's day!"
>
> *You:* "My intention was not to ruin your day. Rather, I think it is a good idea to include our bosses in this conversation as a next step."

An important dimension of this conversation is that the language remains nonjudgmental, meaning you are not using terms such as "manipulative, power-seeking, and passive-aggressive." These are value-laden words that can work against you. People may react to the word instead of the behavior described—and that is not what you want. Instead, describe the behavior and, in this instance, try to quote as accurately as you can remember.

THE BOSS STRATEGY

Of all these difficult conversations, clients have told me that it is giving feedback to the boss that's the hardest. Just as with direct reports and peers, individuals give themselves many messages about this situation—and thus avoid the conversation. Table 3.9 provides some of the top reasons individuals fail to proceed with giving feedback to a boss.

Yes, some of the reasons could be true. So, before embarking on giving feedback to your boss, please remember that the cost-benefit strategy is where you start to discern if you are even going to do this. Table 3.10 provides a dissection of the boss strategy.

TABLE 3.9

Examples of the Top Reasons Individuals Are Reluctant to Provide Feedback to Their Bosses Demonstrating Toxic Behaviors

- "I'll be fired!"
- "She'll watch me like a hawk after this."
- "What if I'm wrong?"
- "Maybe things are not as bad as I think. I've had worse bosses."
- "Others seem to be OK with his behavior."

TABLE 3.10

The Boss Strategy

Be clear about the difficulty of the conversation and empathize regarding the pressures your boss faces (if relevant).

Outline your commitment to your boss and the organization.

State what is bothering you in behaviorally specific terms.

Solicit your boss's thoughts. Listen.

Engage in discussing possible solutions and select the most appropriate option.

See if the boss is willing to follow up.

I have positioned these strategies in order of difficulty: direct report, peer, and finally, boss. If your boss is toxic, your anxiety is likely rising. Take heart. Having a structured method such as this will help. Let us study a case example here and see how it goes:

Be clear about the difficulty of the conversation. Empathize:

> *You:* "Tina, while I have enjoyed working with you over the past year, lately something is getting in the way of our ability to work together effectively. I do understand that you have been under a lot of pressure. I know it must be difficult to manage everything on your plate and, hopefully, this conversation will help us move forward so that we can work as efficiently as possible."

Outline your commitment:

> *You:* "Before I share what is bothering me, I want you to know that I am committed to continuing to be a productive member of your team." (If indeed this is the case based on the results from your cost-benefit strategy.)

State what is bothering you in behavioral terms:

> *You:* "I want to share what has happened in the last two team meetings you have led. In the first one, you asked me to share with the team the detailed estimates of the Eastman project plan. When I shared with you and the team that I was still working on them, you said 'Never mind. I'll do this myself.' You didn't let me finish. I was about to say that while I was still working on the plan, I had some preliminary numbers I would have liked to share. You cut me off. In a follow-up meeting, you shared with the group that you received the numbers but did not agree with them and that I had underestimated the project density. That was the first I had heard of this assessment of yours. Tina, I am committed to this project but in both these situations, it made

me feel undervalued and, just as importantly, that I was not being given a proper chance to explain myself."

Solicit their thoughts:

> *You:* "I welcome your thoughts, Tina."
>
> *Boss:* "When you don't have what I need, I feel you are slacking off. You need to have the numbers and project ideas when I ask for them."
>
> *You:* "When did you ask for these?"
>
> *Boss:* "I just expected you to have them for the meeting."
>
> *You:* "Did you ever tell me this?"
>
> *Boss:* "No, but it was pretty obvious."
>
> *You:* "Not to me."

Engage in discussing possible solutions:

> *You:* "How about this? The next time you need something, please let me know directly. And if I have a hunch you might need these at a certain time, I'll ask."
>
> *Boss:* "Sounds OK to me."
>
> *You:* "One other thing. I don't want to be embarrassed in front of the team. When you say things like, 'I'll just do it myself next time,' that is embarrassing to me and to be honest, quite shaming. I know this is just my feeling. So, what about saying these things to me, but not in front of others. OK?"
>
> *Boss:* "All right."

See if the boss is willing to follow up:

> *You:* "Can we touch base in a couple of weeks after our next two team meetings and see how it goes?"
>
> *Boss:* "Sure."
>
> *You:* "Tina, I want you to know how much I appreciate your listening to me on this important issue for me. I want to continue working well with you."
>
> *Boss:* "I don't completely agree but I will go along with this."
>
> *You:* "Thanks."

As you can see from this conversation, it was relatively positive. However, it is not always this easy. If the conversation does not go in the direction of getting a commitment to change, you should consider the "power in numbers" approach. In working with uncivil people there is often power in numbers when trying to change their behaviors. There are two caveats here. If the behavior is not overly serious, then the first time you have a conversation with your boss, it should be one-on-one. However, if there is either no change in behavior when the person agreed to this or if there is no resolution from the first meeting, bring in another voice. Based on the context of the situation, this could be an individual both of you trust, a human resource professional, or even the boss's boss depending upon the relationship you have with him/her. Bottom line: "Don't go it alone" continuously. Power in numbers is the mantra! Table 3.11 provides a summary of this numbers approach. This may appear as ganging up on the individual, but it is meant to provide you with a less intimidating context. Remember, this person is the boss and, depending upon the context, this could be a highly threatening event. And if the boss remarks that this appears to be a "ganging up" method, I suggest repeating to the boss that it is a way to express feelings in an open, less threatening manner.

> In working with uncivil people there is often power in numbers when trying to change their behaviors. There are two caveats here. If the behavior is not overly serious, then the first time you have a conversation with your boss, it should be one-on-one. However, if there is either no change in behavior when the person agreed to this or if there is no resolution from the first meeting, bring in another voice.

One thing that is helpful when giving feedback to your boss is a good negotiation approach. You need to have a Best Alternative to a Negotiated Agreement—what is referred to in negotiation language as your BATNA (Fisher & Ury, 1981). What this means is that if you do not come to agreement, you need to have something else in your "back pocket." Maybe it is talking with an HR person and engaging him/her in the conversation. Or maybe other team members are having a similar problem, and you can bring them in on the conversation with your boss. Again, power in numbers. Numbers in terms of people to have along when talking with your boss, and numbers in terms of people to help you explore options.

TABLE 3.11

Power-in-Numbers Approach When Giving the Toxic Boss Feedback

- In general, use this for your second attempt at giving the uncivil boss feedback.
- If you are intimidated, more numbers may be useful even on the first attempt at giving feedback.
- Other "voices" to increase the number may be a trusted colleague, a human resource professional, or even the boss's boss.

MIXING AND MATCHING YOUR STRATEGIES

When it comes to human behavior, no one template is going to work 100 percent of the time. That is why I tell my clients to feel comfortable "mixing and matching" the various strategies outlined here. For example, you may find something in the boss strategy useful with a peer. Or something in the direct report strategy that could be effective with your boss.

Because of the difficulty of these types of conversations, it is very easy to avoid them—putting them off while hoping the situation gets better on its own. Consider Table 3.12, which identifies some of these avoidance messages we give ourselves. Simply ask yourself this question: Are these avoidance behaviors appropriate, or are these behaviors excuses? To help you determine the power of these messages, I have designed an assessment survey for you to complete.

I have created this informal assessment survey to help people begin understanding that they might be "catastrophizing" the situation and that they do have some power. By considering the opposite of conversation avoiders, you will be better positioned to take actions that make a difference.

Hopefully, some of these positively framed thoughts will spur on actually having a conversation with the toxic person. Unfortunately, many individuals just simply do not know how to start the conversation because of its potentially explosive situation. Therefore, I recommend some conversation starters that will enhance the intent of the conversation (Table 3.13). You will see from these starters that they are not completely blunt, but also do not sidestep the issue. When these conversation starters are used to initiate the feedback conversation, you will find a more productive and efficient outcome.

Just as conversation starters can help percolate and jump-start the conversation, I have found that many people have trouble ending the conversation with a toxic person. Therefore, in Table 3.14, I have created some sample conversation enders. As with any kind of a template, you have to be judicious in tailoring this to your own needs. Being genuine is key. Therefore, feel free to revise any of these endings to accommodate your personal need along with your own genuine style of delivery.

This chapter should help you become much more comfortable with these strategic conversations. Having a structured plan of action will help you be much more comfortable with providing feedback, as well as having a

TABLE 3.12

Assessment Survey of Conversation Avoidance Behaviors

For those who have wanted to give a toxic person feedback but have stalled, please consider completing this survey. Color in the circle corresponding with the response that most closely matches what you say to yourself before you attempt giving feedback to the person.

	Not Characteristic of Me	Somewhat Characteristic of Me	Highly Characteristic of Me
1. "This is way too uncomfortable for me."	O	O	O
2. "This is HR's (or someone else's) job."	O	O	O
3. "I don't have the time."	O	O	O
4. "If I say something, things could get worse."	O	O	O
5. "Nothing will change. I'll keep my mouth shut."	O	O	O
6. "I won't know what to do if he flies off the handle."	O	O	O
7. "The person could do something to get back at me."	O	O	O
8. "I should have done this a year ago. It's too late."	O	O	O
9. "It's really not that bad. I'll just stay the course."	O	O	O
10. "I'll continue to talk it over with others."	O	O	O

When assessing your results, I suggest you do the following:

1. See if there are one or two quotes in the "highly characteristic of me" category.
2. Then, analyze the "highly characteristic" quote(s), using the following criteria:
   a. Turn the quote around to the opposite. For example:
      i. "I don't have the time." ➔ "I do have the time."
      ii. "I won't know what to do if he flies off the handle." ➔ "I will be prepared if he flies off the handle."
      iii. "It's really not that bad. I'll just stay the course." ➔ "It is a pretty bad situation. I need to do something."

(Continued)

TABLE 3.12 (CONTINUED)

Assessment Survey of Conversation Avoidance Behaviors

    b. Then, fill in the missing pieces with each of these opposites. For example:
       i. "I do have the time. This is important to me. I have complained about it long enough. I need to put a stake in the ground. I'll present several 30-minute times to Bess and see what times might work for her to have a conversation with me."
      ii. "I do know what I can do if he flies off the handle. If he gets abusive, I can tell him that when he calms down I'll continue the conversation. Or I can simply tell him that I need to leave but I would follow up later and see if he wants to continue the conversation. Or I can simply leave and ask HR to accompany me to facilitate the next meeting with him."
     iii. "It is a pretty bad situation. I need to do something. I will talk with HR about how best to position this conversation."
  3. Please refer to Table 3.13 immediately following this section for feedback conversation starters.

TABLE 3.13

Feedback Conversation Starters

Because of the threatening and intimidating behaviors that are indicative of many toxic individuals, some of us have a hard time starting the conversation. There are no easy approaches; however, having some planned ways to initiate the conversation can ease the burden and produce greater effectiveness. Here are some conversation starters for you to consider. Adapt them to your own needs and special situations.

- "I'd like to talk with you about (fill in the situation). We may have different views about this and I'd like to present mine and then ask for your thoughts."
- "We've had some difficulties over the past few weeks and I'd like to reach a better understanding about how we might approach this."
- "I need your thoughts on what just happened this morning. When might you have a few minutes to discuss this?"
- "I'd like to chat with you about something that I think will help us work more effectively together."
- "I noticed that we have different views about this situation and I want to talk with you about my concerns here."
- "Lately, something is getting in the way of us working together effectively."

more successful outcome once the feedback has been given. And hopefully, as you have seen, the structures here are meant as prompts, not to be followed in any rote kind of way. By adding your own spin to the conversation, you will improve you chance of success in providing feedback to a toxic individual.

TABLE 3.14

Feedback Conversation Enders

Just as it can be difficult to start a conversation with a toxic individual, many clients of mine have reported the same for how to end the conversation. Here are some for you to consider and adapt to tailor to your own circumstances.

- "Right now I am not sure where this will go, but I want to relate to you that I am glad we talked."
- "If I could do this all over again, I wish we had this discussion sooner instead of later. But I am pleased as to where we are going now."
- "I believe that if we had not talked, our relationship would have deteriorated further and it could have jeopardized others, including ourselves. I am glad we talked."
- "I appreciate your being open for this discussion. It was not pleasant for either of us. I am hopeful for our positive work together in the future."
- "Even though we did not accomplish all that we set out to today with this conversation, I see this as a starting point for our effective work together in the future."

4

How We Enable Toxic Behaviors to Persist

Some of us enable people to get away with bad behavior. As in many enabling systems, there are those who are aware of the behavior of a toxic individual; others may not be. In either case, these enablers contribute to the problem by allowing the behavior to continue. Consider this non-work example as a way to introduce the concept of enabling—an example that unfortunately occurs in some families with a chemically addicted family member. With an addicted teen, siblings may find excuses that prolong the addiction (e.g., "Sarah is under a lot stress about getting into college, so I better not call her on her behavior."). Parents may be equally to blame (e.g., "We'll allow Sarah to violate curfew one more time because this is a special circumstance."). Giving Sarah just one more chance is enabling behavior. Our research found that this same form of enabling behavior occurs in organizations; we call these enablers *toxic protectors* and *toxic buffers* (Kusy & Holloway, 2009).

TOXIC PROTECTORS AND TOXIC BUFFERS

Toxic protectors are those individuals who receive some benefit from the toxic person's behavior and therefore enable it to continue. From the research Dr. Elizabeth Holloway and I conducted, we found the benefits stem from three primary sources:

- A social relationship
- Productivity
- Performance

The *social relationship protector* enables the uncivil person's behavior because of the relationship the enabler has with the toxic individual. Whether the social relationship is a friendship, a club acquaintance, a workout partner, or any other social context, social protectors give added leeway to toxic people. Table 4.1 summarizes some of the types of individuals who could be social relationship protectors.

> Toxic protectors are those individuals who receive some benefit from the toxic person's behavior and therefore enable it to continue.

The *productivity protector* allows the person to get away with toxic behavior because of her/his high level of productivity. The typical scenario here is the situation where the person's performance brings in money, resources, or needed services. With a recent client of mine, the person was the top physician as identified through her role in having the most patients, bringing in prestige to the organization, and taking in the most money. But she was still a toxic person! This presents a difficult situation, particularly if the boss is a protector because the boss protector has a lot at stake in making sure this individual does not quit. So, the boss may protect by not providing realistic performance reviews—skating over the issues the individual presents to others on the team. Table 4.2 describes the various types of variables associated with the productivity protector.

TABLE 4.1

Types of Individuals Who Could Be Social Relationship Protectors of Toxic People

- Friend
- Workout partner at the gym
- Professional association member
- Lunch partner at work
- Member of same faith-based organization

TABLE 4.2

Examples of the Factors Associated with the Productivity Protector

Productivity protectors act for several reasons, the most common of which are listed among the following items. These individuals protect because the toxic person brings in such things as:

- Needed organizational income
- Special services
- Material resources
- Cost savings

The third type is the *expertise protector*. Here, the toxic person excels in bringing a special expertise to the organization. With one of my clients, it was an engineer who was renowned in her discipline. How does one compete with this? It's not really productivity that the individual brings; rather she may have special talent in sharing with others her expertise—that brings value to the organization. "What if he/she quits if I say too much as the person's boss?" This is a paradox but one that can be addressed in effective ways, which I will discuss later in this chapter. Table 4.3 delineates what motivates the expertise protector.

The *toxic buffer* has different modus operandi from the toxic protector. The toxic buffer is the individual who sees the impact of the person's behavior and does something proactively to minimize its negative effects on others. Unfortunately, their "proactive" strategies are largely ineffective in the long run, allowing the person to continue their bad behavior. One of the key ways a buffer does this is through organizational restructure. I liken this to when I was in grade school and the teacher had the all-powerful "seating plan." Let us say Mitch is seated in the back of the room and has been labeled the "troublemaker." What does the teacher do? Move Mitch to the front of the room so the teacher can keep an eye on him. What happens next? Mitch is likely to demonstrate good behavior when the teacher is looking. But when the teacher's head is turned or leaves the room, Mitch's behavior reverts to the same mischievous stuff. This is exactly what can happen with an organizational restructure. For example, the person may have significant responsibilities removed from her plate, may be placed in a different office removed from the day-to-day workings with team members, or may even have their direct reports now report to another individual— all with the intent of buffering the team from the person's antics. But does it really? Read on.

TABLE 4.3

Example of What Motivates the Expertise Protector

The expertise protector enables the uncivil person to get away with bad behavior for several reasons. The toxic person may possess:
- A special talent
- Unique experiences that no one else possesses
- Expertise that would be too expensive to bring in from the outside
- A background that has value to the organization's success

The *toxic buffer* has different modus operandi from the toxic protector. The toxic buffer is the individual who sees the impact of the person's behavior and does something proactively to lessen its negative impact on others. Unfortunately, their "proactive" strategies are largely ineffective in the long run, allowing the person to continue their bad behavior.

Often, if a leader restructures a team to accommodate a toxic person, all hell breaks loose. This is what occurred with a client about a year ago. Rather than dealing with the person's behavior head-on, the boss reconfigured the department such that she removed direct report responsibilities from the person—making him an "individual contributor." What happened? First, the rest of the team viewed this as allowing the person to get away with bad behavior. Second, the team also saw this as a way for him to get the same pay without having to supervise anyone. Needless to say, it proved fruitless and after much unneeded consternation, the person was fired because their toxic behavior continued in spite of the organizational restructure.

ARE YOU A TOXIC PROTECTOR?

As they say on the metaphorical therapy "couch," awareness is the first action needed to change behavior. This section will help you better understand whether you are a toxic protector or toxic buffer. If so, you can do something about it. To understand if you are a toxic protector, take the following quiz (Table 4.4). Hopefully, this provides some additional insights that may call for further action on your part.

This quiz is one that will hopefully provide insights on corrective actions, should you be a toxic protector. You cannot change behavior if you are not aware it is occurring.

ARE YOU A TOXIC BUFFER?

Unlike the toxic protector whose motivation is based on gaining something from the person—whether it be a special relationship, productivity, or expertise—the toxic buffer is motivated to protect others from

TABLE 4.4

"Are You a Toxic Protector?" Quiz

To help you determine if you have toxic protector tendencies, please color in the circle corresponding with your response. This instrument is intended for those who are currently working with a toxic person or have worked with one in the past. As you respond to this quiz, please keep this toxic person in mind when responding to each item.

With the toxic person I have in mind, how characteristic of me is each of the following behaviors:

	Not Characteristic of Me	Somewhat Characteristic of Me	Highly Characteristic of Me
1. I ignored the person's behavior.	O	O	O
2. I used my special relationship with them as an excuse to do nothing.	O	O	O
3. Because the person increased organizational productivity, I chose to do nothing in spite of the disruptive behavior continuing.	O	O	O
4. Considering the person's high level of expertise, it was better for me to let it go.	O	O	O
5. I had authority to do something about their toxic behavior but I did not do anything.	O	O	O
6. I have taken the side of the person against my better judgment.	O	O	O
7. I have taken little proactive actions at work about the person's behavior.	O	O	O
8. I have not shared my concerns with anyone who had the authority to do something about the toxic person.	O	O	O

To assess your results, consider the following:

1. *Identify characteristic behaviors.* First, what are your most characteristic behaviors that allow the person to get away with acting poorly?
2. *Check it out with others.* Ask someone who knows you well and is knowledgeable about the person's behavior if they have seen you as a toxic protector. If so, in what ways?
3. *Listen* to their responses. Do not interrupt.
4. *Act.* Come up with a plan of action based on the content in the section of this chapter entitled "What to Do if You Are a Toxic Protector or Buffer."

the antics of the uncivil person. Often with high emotional intelligence, buffers are very good at circumventing the toxic person's behavior when it comes to the forefront. In Table 4.5 you will see a quiz that will hopefully enhance your insights regarding whether you are a toxic buffer.

TABLE 4.5

"Are You a Toxic Buffer?" Quiz

To help you determine if you have toxic buffer tendencies, please color in the circle corresponding with your response. This instrument only works if you are currently working with a toxic person or have worked with one in the past. If either of these scenarios is true, then please keep this person in mind when responding to each item.

With the toxic person I have in mind, how characteristic is each of the following behaviors:

	Not Characteristic of Me	Somewhat Characteristic of Me	Highly Characteristic of Me
1. Have tried to "soften the toxic person's blow" on others	O	O	O
2. Made excuses for the toxic behavior	O	O	O
3. Tried to convince others the value the person brings to the organization	O	O	O
4. Have chosen not to give the person direct feedback about the person's behavior	O	O	O
5. If having the authority to do so, removed responsibilities from the person to allow this individual to continue without other intervention	O	O	O
6. Did not share with my boss the impact of the person's behavior on others	O	O	O

To assess these results, consider the following:

1. *Get unbiased feedback.* Show an uncompleted version of this quiz to someone who knows you well and knows of the toxic person. Ask this person to rate you on each of the items.
2. *Identify behaviors of which you are least proud.* Referring to the items graded "highly characteristic of me," of which are you the least proud?
3. *Compare and discuss deviations.* Compare their responses to yours. Discuss any deviations without trying to sway their thinking.
4. *Act.* Come up with a plan of action based on the content of the section entitled "What to Do if You Are a Toxic Protector or Buffer."

WHAT TO DO IF YOU ARE A TOXIC PROTECTOR OR BUFFER

First, there is good news if you are a toxic protector or toxic buffer! Protectors and buffers are often open to receiving feedback about the impact of their behavior on others. In fact, I have found that sometimes they welcome this because they are relieved that they do not have to continue on this path. There's a lot of anxiety associated with maneuvering in this way. Therefore, if there are items on which you have scored "highly characteristic of me," consider this your awareness-generating feedback. Before making any assumptions, be sure to have a conversation with either the person who completed this quiz with you, or with someone who knows this situation very well. Then, if it appears you are a toxic protector or buffer, consider doing the following:

1. *Seek information from others.* Review previous data that others have given you that you are enabling the person to get away with bad behavior.
2. *Identify themes.* Determine if there is a theme here based on a pattern of behavior that is repeated.
3. *Make it a goal to stop at least one enabling behavior.* Identify at least one behavior you will attempt to stop that will lessen the enabling process. Do not be absolute here; what we know about behavioral changes is that "baby steps" are key. One behavior change—not several—is the mantra!
4. *Share your goal with one person you trust.* As appropriate, share with a trusted individual what you intend to do. This fourth step is a critical one because there is research that demonstrates if you make a goal public, there is a higher probability you will achieve it. So, stating to another individual your potential action will increase the probability of success. Be very careful here about not gossiping about the individual. Remember, this is about *you* and what *you* will stop doing.

Following these four steps will help you better understand your enabling role, as well as the behavior *you* will need to change. Working with protector or buffer clients I have coached, I have discovered that both hearing and doing something about this is not easy, because these individuals have invested a lot of time and energy into enabling. However, once they make a decision to do something about it, success can be swift and effective.

WHAT TO DO IF SOMEONE ELSE IS A TOXIC PROTECTOR OR BUFFER

Since toxic protectors and buffers are much more open to feedback than toxic people, you can capitalize on this statistic if you see someone who is either a toxic protector or buffer. In this way, you could be the catalyst who indirectly helps challenge the person to new behaviors. Here's a clear strategy for engaging toxic protectors or buffers in understanding how their behaviors enable toxic individuals:

1. *Sensitivity with focus.* First, be sensitive. Many protectors and buffers are doing what they think is right in order to keep the status quo and not upset the "apple cart." Be gentle but direct; focus on the behavior—the toxic person's as well as the toxic protector/buffer.
2. *Engagement.* Second, ask for the person's perspectives on this situation.
3. *Statistics with impact.* Third, gently synthesize some of the statistics about the impact toxic people have on performance (see the statistics identified in Chapter 2). It's important that you not come off like a robot reciting statistics. Instead, identify a few statistics that you believe could be relevant in your situation, and share an overall message about how this kind of behavior can impact such things as team performance, safety, and turnover.
4. *Act.* Fourth, do something. Suggest actions as appropriate and relevant.
5. *Closing.* Fifth, as you close the conversation, share that you understand that the protector or buffer has been attempting to manage a trying situation. Thank the individual for being open to the conversation and share that you would be willing to talk at another time regarding any questions or concerns.

Going through each of these steps a bit more closely may help get a better feel for this important strategy. In terms of the first step of sensitivity, it is important to be gentle. The protector or buffer has likely spent a great deal of time in trying to keep the status quo and in keeping the toxic behavior to a manageable level. Engage in the second step. In the third step, share a synthesis of relevant statistics of the impact toxic people have on others. Do not overpower here. When you share your own observations, as well as those of others in the third step, be concrete and behaviorally specific. And do not gossip. When you suggest actions in the fourth step, offer just a few ways in which you may help. Do not inundate with many strategies. Keep it simple. Finally, as you close the conversation, affirm that you understand that the protector or buffer has been trying to manage an unsettling situation. Thank the person for this but do not be overly placating. Relate that you hope this conversation will bring the protector or buffer's behavior into a new direction.

Here's a sample coaching conversation I recently had with a client related to this strategy:

1. *Sensitivity with focus:*

   Mitch: "You've talked with me a few times now about how it's so hard to hold this team together because of Dave shaming people in meetings, putting down others one-on-one, and taking credit for the team's work as his own. I know this puts you in a vulnerable position of feeling you have to take responsibility for Dave's behavior because he is such a high producer. Cathy, I believe you do not need to take on this extra burden to your already overloaded schedule. The work that you have put into restructuring this team because of one person is noble but fruitless. It has not stopped Dave's behavior and, in fact, has begun to alienate your team members from you. I recall you mentioned to me that you were concerned that several team members are no longer coming to you with problems they are having on your big Signature Project."

2. *Engagement:*

   Mitch: "What do you think, Cathy?"

   Cathy: "I know you're right but I just can't get out of my head the fact that Dave always hits his targeted goals. Not just hits, but surpasses by a long shot! I don't know what I'd do without him."

   Mitch: First, you might get a better night's sleep, and so would your team members!

   Cathy: (Nervous laugh.)

3. *Statistics with impact:*

> *Mitch:* "Cathy, I want you to think about the impact of Dave's behavior on not just you and your team, but the organization as well. In several studies, researchers have demonstrated the negative effects of toxic people. Such as individual team members who may have quit as a result. The cost of interviewing, replacing, and retraining new members can be astounding. Not to mention the sleepless nights you are having! Add to all this the team members who actually avoid Dave and spend less time at work. Just the other day you said you were concerned because two of your team members are coming in later and leaving earlier without any indication of bringing their work home."

> *Cathy:* I know. It's just that it's such a busy time of year and I don't even think my boss is aware of how devastating this has been for my team and me.

> *Mitch:* "It's not surprising that your boss isn't fully aware of Dave's impact on others and this organization. Your boss Shelley sees Dave as a star because you have protected her from truly understanding the impact of Dave's behavior. Dave seems to blend into the fold instead of coming to Shelly's attention! Just like you protected the team from Dave with your recent reorganization, you also protected your boss from Dave."

4. *Act:*

> *Mitch:* "I wonder what would happen if you decided to stop protecting Dave? Maybe start, in a small way, when he belittles people at a meeting, call him on it then—not later. It's important for the team to hear publicly that you will not allow this. For example, the next time he tells someone on the team that 'she is so far off base that many have stopped listening to her', consider responding with something like this: 'First, Dave, that is absolutely not true. In fact, others have related to me how important this person has been for the success of the Signature Project. Second, and even more importantly, I will not allow anyone talking to others on the team in this way.'"

> *Cathy:* "You want me to do this in front of everyone?"

> *Mitch:* "Yes. It's not meant to shame Dave. Rather, it's a way to demonstrate to the team that you support them and will not allow this kind of behavior. But if you are concerned about this

public context, you can certainly start with having the same conversation with Dave one-on-one."

5. *Closing:*

    Mitch: "I hope you'll give this a try for your sake and the team's. Just remember the amount of time this has consumed. Keep in mind those statistics. In addition, please remember you have a great human resources department here; they can help you further process this. Of course, I'm available and would like to hear how it goes."

    Cathy: "Thanks, Mitch. I'll give it a try by first talking with Dave one-on-one. In addition, I'll ask for HR's support before doing this. I'll keep in touch with you and let you know how it went. Great idea about talking with human resources, I don't know why I didn't think of this!"

GETTING OUT OF BEING STUCK

I hope that the quizzes and templates in this chapter help those of you who are stuck in protecting or buffering a toxic person. What has been fascinating to me as both an organizational consultant and coach is the power these simple strategies have in moving someone forward with clear, proactive, and concrete actions. One of the clear themes I hope you identify in this chapter is the power of identifying a person you can trust. Engaging someone else both as a confidant and someone who can help you check out your perspectives is powerful. Do not feel you have "to go it" alone. Table 4.6 identifies some of the things you should consider in establishing trust with a confidant regarding your being a protector or buffer.

One important factor in this assessment is that you need to feel comfortable with the confidant. In this way, responses to the questions are likely to be more valuable. Let's examine each of these questions. Regarding the first question (Can this confidant be objective in helping me assess the situation?), if the person cannot be objective you then need to address the issue of their subjectivity and make an informed decision whether this is the best person with whom to share your thoughts about being a toxic protector or buffer.

As far as the second question is concerned (If he/she has seen me interact with the toxic person, will he/she give me honest feedback?), it is important

TABLE 4.6

Key Questions a Protector or Buffer Should Consider in Finding a Confidant to Share Their Protection or Buffering Roles

---

- Can this confidant be objective in helping me assess the situation?
- If he/she has seen me interact with the toxic person, will he/she give me honest feedback?
- Does this person have a connection with the toxic person that could influence our discussion?
- How effective are this person's listening skills?

---

that this person give you direct feedback. You do not want someone who is going to be hesitant out of fear of offending you.

With the third question (Does this person have a connection with the toxic person that could influence our discussion?), the key is to assess her/his honesty. For example, if they have a connection to the toxic person, will this connection influence their advice? It is not necessarily bad that she/he has a connection with the toxic person. What *is* important is that she/he owns this and there is a dialog between you and her/him about this. And interestingly, with this connection you may discover that some of *your* behaviors, if alleviated, which could tone down the situation.

Considering the fourth question (How effective are this person's listening skills?), is the confidant able to do some of the following that are demonstrative of good listening skills? Paraphrasing thoughts of others effectively? Waiting and not finishing another person's thoughts?

In any of these four questions, you may not get all the "perfect" answers. Perfection here is not absolute. What is important is that you receive answers that will help you trust that this individual has your best interests at heart.

5

Hiring and Exiting Practices
That Address Toxic Behaviors

Hiring is part art, part science. Unfortunately, many leaders rely primarily on "gut feeling" to make some of the most important decisions for their organizations. Pushing the envelope even further, "gut-feeling" hiring decisions can open a negative floodgate for people to enter your organization. Consider the research conducted by Fernandez-Araoz, Groysberg and Nohria, (2009), where they found that 50 percent of hiring managers relied mainly on "gut feeling" and selected candidates based on "what it took" to be effective in almost any job recruitment. This is a very important statistic, demonstrating that toxic people can easily slip through the cracks unless a structured, concrete, and due diligent hiring process is put in place. Relying primarily on "gut feeling" is not advisable. Just as alarming is their finding that 43 percent of executive search consultants reported that, for their clients, number of years of experience was one of the top reasons for offering a position to a candidate. However, only 24 percent of their clients gave the same weight to the candidate's ability to collaborate in teams. By devaluing this team collaboration behavior, job candidates who might not work well with others are given far more consideration than they deserve. Therefore, it is incumbent on hiring managers and hiring teams to pay more attention to the teamwork aspects of the hiring process.

At the other end of the spectrum is a practice called "the exit interview." Unfortunately, many organizations get failing grades in conducting and documenting exit interviews. In this chapter, I will address how to improve your recruiting and hiring practices, as well as your exit interview methods—with a focus on how these can be astoundingly successful ways to understand and deal with toxic people.

Unfortunately, many organizations get failing grades in conducting and documenting exit interviews. Pushing the envelope even further, "gut-feeling" hiring decisions can open a negative floodgate for people to enter your organization.

A POORLY MANAGED RECRUITING PROCESS

This case occurred a few years ago with one of my clients, a leader who believed she had captured the essence of a good team interview process. For the sake of example, I have changed slightly some of the titles and contexts so as not to breach any confidentiality surrounding this serious recruiting error. Theresa, VP of Operations, had assembled her leadership team to design the interview process. Two components were incorporated here: structured questions designed to get at the "meat" of the job and all leadership team members being asked for their input into questions. In addition, they had planned a casual lunch and dinner with the candidate to allow opportunities for more candid questions to emerge. Seems appropriate and relevant. Right? Good so far! But here is how the events actually occurred.

Theresa had an appointment conflict and was running late and could not be at the airport to greet the candidate. So, her administrative assistant volunteered to go in her absence. The candidate, Adele, was greeted at the airport by Peter, the administrative assistant. Trying to engage Adele in conversation, Peter was surprised that Adele said very little. Peter's questions were met with one-sentence answers and nothing more. So Peter, being the astute person he is, tried more open-ended questions designed to spur on the conversation. Still, one-sentence responses. Further, Adele did not try to initiate any conversation designed to show interest in the position. Logically, Peter assumed that Adele was nervous. After all, this is a very important position in the organization. Peter thought this to be the case until the hiring manager, Theresa, arrived. What happened next was quite a shock to Peter. Adele morphed into an exuberant, effusive, and eloquent conversationalist!

The cause for her change in demeanor was clear: it was about power. Adele perceived that Theresa had the power to make decisions; Peter did not. So, Adele committed a serious misstep: she "kissed up" to Theresa and "knocked down" to Peter, as I have described in previous chapters in this book—the chameleon effect in action! And those who "knock down and kiss up" have a high probability of being toxic persons. You do not want these folks entering your organization.

Unfortunately, this story did not end well. Peter never shared his concerns; Theresa and the recruiting team hired Adele. It was a year of hell for the team and the organization where people found it very difficult to work with Adele. Eventually, she was fired. Another sad part of this story is that this could have been prevented. What could have been done proactively to reduce the probability of this kind of a power play going unnoticed by leaders? It is a very simple, inexpensive strategy that I call the *recruiting cue sheet.*

THE RECRUITING CUE SHEET

The next time you are in hiring mode, go beyond the immediate interviewing team to others who have a casual opportunity to interact with the candidate. The individuals could be receptionists, maintenance people, and cafeteria workers—anyone who could possibly come in contact with the candidate. Consider the wider organizational team with the help of the *recruiting cue sheet* in Table 5.1. Here, the hiring manager would present the recruiting cue sheet to these other individuals. As you can see, the *recruiting cue sheet* is simple but direct; the end goal is improving the hiring process by not hiring a toxic person.

Use this cue sheet to help you discern the multiple ways someone presents themselves during the interviewing process. Distribute this recruiting cue sheet to those who are not formally part of the interviewing process, but still might have an opportunity to interact with the candidate. Here are the instructions followed by the potential items on which a candidate could be assessed.

The hiring manager should consider a variety of individuals who may have interactions with the candidate. For example, people who work in an array of departments such as food service, maintenance, reception, as well as administrative assistants—anyone who would have an opportunity to casually meet the candidate. Based on my experiences, you may be surprised to find data that both corroborate those of the hiring team and run counter to this team's assessment. Consider all data and if there are views that run counter to the hiring team's experiences, gather more data and, if necessary, conduct more interviews. Please consider the scenario in which Adele was hired. While I can't say for sure if this kind of process would have prevented her from being hired, I can affirm that it would have significantly reduced the probability of

TABLE 5.1

The Recruiting Cue Sheet Template

Our department is hiring a (position title inserted here). To help make a successful hire, we need your help. On (select date), we will be interviewing (name of candidate) for this position. At this time, you may or may not have an opportunity to meet (name of candidate). We hope you do and, if so, we want your feedback on this form. The questions are straightforward and designed to add an extra layer of feedback that would be difficult for us to obtain, since your interaction would occur during casual times. Please color in the circle that applies most to the situation, as well as provide your personal views in the comments section for each question. When our formal interviewing process ends, I will collect this form from you and review your responses with the hiring team. These responses are confidential in the sense that we will only share these with the hiring team—not the candidate and not your boss unless your boss is part of the hiring team. Please note that we are asking several people to do this, so your feedback would not be the only one we are collecting. I ask that you keep this sheet away from the view of (name of candidate), so as not to make (name of candidate) needlessly nervous.

	Minimally or Not at All	Somewhat	To a Large Extent
1. How did the candidate engage you in conversation?	O	O	O
Comments:			
2. How did the candidate demonstrate any of our organizational values?	O	O	O
Comments:			
3. Did the candidate seem to be the kind of co-worker with whom you would like to work?	O	O	O
Comments:			
4. What else do you believe might be important for us to know that has not been captured by these three questions?			

Thank you for completing this form. I will plan on collecting this by the end of the day on (provide date).

TABLE 5.2

Potential Individuals Who Can Provide Insight about a Candidate
during the Recruiting Process

- Maintenance professionals
- Cafeteria personnel
- Administrative assistants
- Receptionists
- Security staff
- Drivers

a bad hire had the administrative assistant, Peter, been asked for his opinion. This cue sheet will significantly reduce the probability of hiring a toxic person. Table 5.2 identifies a list of individuals I have found influential in enhancing the interviewing process through the recruiting cue sheet.

A variation of this strategy of informal assessors is to have a meal with the candidate and observe how she interacts with the server. Does the candidate treat him respectfully? If there is an order mix-up, how does the candidate handle this? Of course, because the candidate may be nervous, this may not be the best opportunity to observe their manners. But it may provide a hint of what the person would be like as a colleague.

THE DANGER OF HYPOTHETICAL QUESTIONS

Despite all the best intentions, many leaders give little thought to the format of their interview questions. One basic error in format is asking hypothetical questions. These allow candidates to again slip through the cracks—especially those who are capable of "knocking down and kissing up." How do hypothetical questions allow people to hide information important for the hiring team? Think about asking a candidate to share his/her experiences in managing a disruptive and unproductive team. Now, let us pretend this candidate is toxic. Rather than share these team problems and possibly expose the invulnerabilities the candidate has had with the team and rather than directly lying about it and creating a rosy scenario (and possibly getting caught in a lie), the candidate presents to the interviewer hypothetical situations. If the individual did not have positive experiences with the team, then it is much easier to say what she *would* do instead of getting caught in a lie by framing something that the individual has done but did not do. Ahead are two tables. One contains a set of hypothetical questions, and in the next box the same questions reframed in a more useful way. What I have found in my own consulting practice is that some candidates turn non-hypothetical questions into hypothetical ones. Toxic people who are trying to hide something do this frequently. It is a form of lying in which they hide their real actions behind a hypothetical screen. For a sampling of hypothetical questions, please refer to Table 5.3. These are the questions that should be avoided during an interview. Examples of non-hypothetical questions—which should be engaged during the interviewing process—are listed in Table 5.4.

It should be kept in mind that even the best of non-hypothetical questions could generate hypothetical responses, particularly if someone is trying to hide something from the interviewer. If this should occur, Table 5.5 describes some potential ways to redirect the conversation so that there is an increased probability of generating more revealing responses.

> Despite all the best intentions, many leaders give little thought to the format of their interview questions. One basic error in format is asking hypothetical questions. These allow candidates to slip through the cracks—especially those who are capable of "knocking down and kissing up."

TABLE 5.3

Common Hypothetical Questions, Which Should Be Avoided during the Interviewing Process

1. "How would you handle a difficult, key customer with whom you disagree?"
2. "How would you deal with a peer with whom you have a conflict?"
3. "How could you work with a direct report who has violated one of our organization's values?"
4. "How should you talk with a peer whom you understand has gossiped about you?"

TABLE 5.4

Examples of Non-Hypothetical Questions, Which Will Increase the Probability of Robust, Meaningful Responses

1. "Please share a recent experience in which you had a difficult, key customer disagree with you. How did you handle this?"
2. "Please consider a situation involving a peer with whom you had conflict. What was the conflict about? How did you try to manage or resolve this?"
3. "Have you ever had a direct report who violated the organizational values? If so, what did you do?"
4. "I want you to recall a situation where you discovered that someone was gossiping about you. What did you do?"

TABLE 5.5

Cues to Handle Candidates Who Answer Non-Hypothetical Questions
with Hypothetical Responses

In this scenario, consider that you have asked a non-hypothetical question but have
received a hypothetical response. Here are some prompts in how to redirect the
conversation as to produce more robust information.

1. "You provided what you would do. I would like you to now take us through this
   process step by step."
2. "You are telling me what you *would* do. Please tell us what you actually did."
3. "We understand how important it is for you to want to make a positive impression
   with us. However, we want to hear what you actually did. Do not worry if you did
   not do this correctly. We all make mistakes. We want to hear your honest response."

ANALYZING RESPONSES FROM CANDIDATE INTERVIEWS

In an article I had coauthored—intended for organization development
professionals—I suggested a three-step process for analyzing responses to
questions posed to executives (Nekoranec & Kusy, 2005). I believe these
same questions are useful in the context of interviewing candidates for
a position. I translate this same process here to reduce the probability of
hiring toxic people:

1. Listen for themes.
2. Explore differences of opinion.
3. Provide follow-up questions.

In this three-step process, each interviewer brings their thoughts
according to these three prompts. To keep the process as valid as
possible, I suggest that each interviewer come prepared with written
responses to these three prompts. This reduces the probability of one's
responses being overly influenced by others during the team discussion
of the candidate.

Interviewing themes emerge in two ways. In the first, an interviewing
team member determines the themes heard among the various answers
given by the candidate. In the second, the entire interviewing team meets
and discusses the themes they have heard collectively. Differences of opinion may certainly occur among team members. These should be discussed
openly. One of the problems I have discovered when recruiting teams
come together is that they often do not know what constitutes a theme.

TABLE 5.6

Perspectives on What Makes Collective Responses into a Theme for the Recruiting Process

---

Sometimes themes are difficult to discern, especially when others ask how you arrived at a theme. I have found these perspectives helpful.

- It is a perspective of at least 50% of the team
- There are several members who believe others beyond the team would find the perspectives critical
- Someone believes that others beyond the interviewing team would push this beyond the 50% mark
- While below the 50% mark, the issue is so important to consider that one person convinces the others that this is a theme and should be addressed

---

Table 5.6 delineates some of the perspectives a team may wish to consider that collapses collective responses into themes.

> Interviewing themes emerge in two ways. In the first, an interviewing team member determines the themes heard among the various answers given by the candidate. In the second, the entire interviewing team meets and discusses the themes they have heard collectively.

The final phase engages potential follow-up questions that need to be asked based on additional information associated with both themes and differences of opinion. Because of the power of "groupthink" in which the sentiment of a critical mass of the group sways members who are in the minority opinion, it is important that people be encouraged to share their written responses. An alternative strategy is for the leader to ask an unbiased person who is not part of the interviewing team to compile all the data into one document without names. This is then shared with the entire team.

What I have discovered most effective with follow-up questions is to be very concrete. Ask for examples of contradictions observed by the interviewing team. There may be a second round of interviews needed to explore these contradictions. At this point, this should be conducted by people in pairs. This improves the reliability of the process. The contradictions heard are likely to be associated with potential toxic behaviors—it is important to get these out on the table early in the interviewing process so you are less likely to make a faulty hiring decision.

What I have discovered most effective with follow-up questions is to be very concrete. Ask for examples of contradictions observed by the interviewing team. There may be a second round of interviews needed to explore these contradictions. At this point, people in pairs should conduct this. This improves the reliability of the process. The contradictions heard are likely to be associated with potential toxic behaviors—it is important to get these out on the table early in the interviewing process so you are less likely to make a faulty hiring decision.

VARY YOUR INTERVIEWING QUESTIONS

One of the major blunders made in the interviewing process is for interviewers to ask the same questions to the candidates over and over again. This not only creates monotony and fatigue for the interviewee, but it also creates a situation where it easy for the interviewee to learn the best pattern of responses the interviewers might be expecting. Understanding these expectations can seriously sabotage interviewing effectiveness. Instead, it is best to provide each separate interviewee with different questions to garner a comprehensive set of responses. It is certainly fine to have a few interviewers with the same questions to check for reliability of responses. But do not overdo this. With the rich mix of methods discussed in this chapter, you do not need the extensive reliability of the same questions for all interviewers. Table 5.7 provides some ways to vary the interviewing questions.

TABLE 5.7

Ways of Varying Interviewing Questions to Arrive at Patterns That Can Address the Potential of Toxic Behaviors

So that interviewee boredom does not set in—which can cause fatigue and a lack of robust responses—I suggest varying interview questions in the following ways.

- Ask for case examples.
- Give certain questions to different team members.
- Provide questions focusing on strengths and areas for improvement.
- For questions focusing on negative aspects, preface this with the fact that no one is perfect in everything and we expect that there will be some behaviors you are still working on.

CHECK REFERENCES THE RIGHT WAY

Here is another scenario that a client recently related to me about the pain of hiring a toxic person. Again, names have been changed to protect anonymity. Steve believed he did everything the "right way" to assure the best hire possible. In retrospect, he realized that the process broke down during the reference checking. Unfortunately, he found out about this too late. About a year after having to fire Deb, a toxic person, Steve attended a conference in which he ran into one of the references Deb had provided. At this conference, the reference asked how the candidate was doing. Steve said it was a bad hiring decision, but did not go into details. However, Steve did end the conversation with the fact that this reference provided a glowing tribute about the candidate. This is where the story gets interesting. The reference said that this was not the case. When Steve asked what she meant, the reference said, "Steve, you seemed to have had your mind made up when I was trying to tell you about Deb. You would not listen. Every time I attempted to relate how she interacted with the team I had been on, you interjected with the 'but' word—singing her praises with the special expertise she would bring to your organization. I finally gave up." Steve was dumbfounded and as he recalled the conversation, it was all coming back to him. There were red flags he ignored.

So, in your reference checking, please have a structured set of questions you plan to ask. Do not interrupt. If something does not agree with what you and your interviewing team found out, instead of trying to justify it, ask for further clarification. If you hear negative things about the individual, do not sweep these under the rug because so much has been positive up to this point. Bring these issues back to the team. The issues could be insignificant ones, but they could also be associated with a powder keg waiting to explode. If necessary, ask for further references, recommend a follow-up interview to check these things out accordingly, or abort the interviewing process with this candidate. This will likely help steer you potentially clear of a bad hire. Table 5.8 provides some top questions to ask references to discern the potential of toxic behaviors surfacing if this candidate became an employee.

> So, in your reference checking, please have a structured set of questions you plan to ask. Do not interrupt. If something does not agree with what you and your interviewing team found out, instead of trying to justify it, ask for further clarification.

TABLE 5.8

A Selection of Top Questions for References to Discern the Potential of Toxic Behaviors Surfacing If a Candidate Becomes an Employee

- How has this person managed conflict?
- How effective has this person been at building work relationships?
- When possible, how does this person engage others in decision-making?
- If you had hired this person, what would be the first piece of advice you would give during his/her first month of work?
- Why would you hire this person? Why not?

WHEN TRADITIONAL EXIT INTERVIEWS DO NOT WORK

While common, exit interviews sometimes do not accomplish the goal of trying to understand why someone is voluntarily leaving the organization. When are these interviews often fraught with disaster? When the boss is the toxic person. As you will recall, 51 percent of individuals who are targets of incivility believe they will quit (Kusy & Holloway, 2009); 12 percent actually do (Pearson & Porath, 2009). And many times the perpetrator is the boss. Because of the extensive emotional damage to one's self-esteem that may occur in these situations, and the threat that some targets feel, some are not likely to be truthful during the exit interview process when they are still technically employees in the organization. Table 5.9 details some of the times when traditional exit interviews do not work.

The solution to ineffective exit interviews is to conduct the exit interviews anywhere from three to six months *after* the individual has left the organization. How might you do this? You could ask him if the deporting employee would be willing to speak with you in three to six months about their experiences within the organization. You could further share with the employee the questions you intend to ask. I have found that these interviews, occurring after the fact, provide appropriate distance and comfort for the individual— as well as more accurate responses. Think of it this way: If someone is feeling

TABLE 5.9

Times When Traditional Exit Interviews May Not Work

- When the boss is toxic
- When the toxic person has powerful influence
- When an individual has had some performance problems that are exposed as the real reason the person is leaving without attribution to the toxic person

threatened by a boss, responses are likely to be disingenuous to further protect oneself, particularly if there is fear on the part of the exiting individual. One candidate who left the organization and had reported to a toxic boss told me this: "I'm not going to allow this person to ruin my reputation in this city. I'll give them what they want to hear and be done with it."

> The solution to ineffective exit interviews is to conduct the exit interviews anywhere from three to six months *after* the individual has left the organization.

Finally, while it may not need to be stated, but just in case, the boss should *never* conduct the exit interview. Ideally, it is the human resource professional who has the skills to do this. Rely on their expertise. And be sure to have the results from the exit interviews reported to key stakeholders—the boss *and* the boss's boss! Table 5.10 documents the types of questions for the ideal exit interview process that occurs three to six months after the person has exited the organization.

In conclusion, exit interviews are something many people believe they know how to do because they are so simple; this thinking often proves problematic. With a few basic strategies discussed in this chapter, you should be well on your way to understanding toxic behaviors in your organization and then discussing this with key influencers who can help gain a foothold in doing something about it.

TABLE 5.10

Sample Exit Interview Questions

Many individuals conduct exit interviews to focus on why the individual is leaving the organization. The following questions are likely to produce more powerful responses that can help guide the organization in the future, since these are done after the individual has departed the organization.

1. "What were the primary reasons for your leaving our agency?"
2. "If there were negative reasons for your leaving, did you try to share your concerns with anyone prior to your departing? If so, what was the response you received?"
3. "Was there any one person responsible for your leaving?"
4. "What could we have done differently to have kept you as a teacher here?"
5. "How effective was the leadership you received?"
6. "In comparison to where you are now working, are there any special insights you now have about our organization?"
7. "Is there anything that I did not ask you that you believe is important for us to understand about your leaving?"

What does one do with the data generated from the exit interview? One of the best strategies is to bring both the individual who has collected the information and the boss into the conversation. I suggest not accusing but simply stating that this is the feedback received. This behavior is often patterned, but if this is an isolated incident, treat it as awareness-generating. If it is a pattern, determine how the boss wants to address this. There is power in numbers. Do not leave it to the interviewing person alone to determine how to manage this. A team approach may be the call to order.

Exit interviews are something many people believe they know how to do because they are so simple; this thinking often proves problematic.

6

Failures and Triumphs of Performance Management in the Toxic World

This chapter begins with a series of questions I have asked hundreds of leaders at keynote addresses I have given in the past few years. I have asked these leaders to respond with a show of hands:

1. "How many of your organizations have a performance appraisal form?"

    (Approximately 95% of leaders have raised their hands to this question)

2. "Of those of you who have raised your hands, how many of your organizations have the organizational values identified on these forms?"

    (Now, the percentage goes down to about 20%)

3. "Of those who have just raised your hands to this second question, how many of your organizations have a rating scale or some form of assessment in which each employee is evaluated on what they are doing to achieve these values?"

    (Now, the percentage goes to a very low 5%)

Figure 6.1 identifies these percentages associated with engagement of a performance appraisal form, whether the values have been identified on this form, and if the values are assessed.

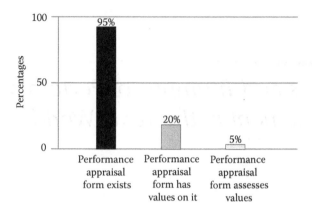

FIGURE 6.1
Percentages of respondents who engage in various performance management practices.

VALUES INTEGRATION AS AN ANTIDOTE TO TOXIC BEHAVIORS

I ask these questions from the previous section because uncivil people are typical violators of organizational values. However, we often do not hold them accountable to these values until it is too late—when leaders are exasperated and at the point of firing them. Unfortunately, it is difficult to fire a high producer (which many toxic people are!)—even though they may violate the organizational values. Why? Because many leaders introduce the values too late into the performance management conversation. And since many uncivil people are clever in maneuvering around this, they will often ask why *they* are being held accountable to these values while others are not. And they're right to wonder! Table 6.1 provides four summary points regarding the significance of the integration of values into performance management.

Leaders need to make the organizational values come alive in the performance management process. If the values are so darned important, then hold *everyone* accountable for achieving these—not just toxic people. Leaders do not necessarily need to get anyone's permission to do this (i.e., HR), although it would be great if HR were on board. For example, leaders may elect to have performance discussions with their employees and require that at least part of the employees' evaluations includes how

TABLE 6.1

Four Reasons for Integrating Your Organization's Values into Your Performance Management Process

---

1. Toxic people often violate organizational values.
2. Everyone should be held accountable to the organizational values in a formal way through the performance management process.
3. When toxic people get out of hand, sometimes it is hard to fire them because they often lament that no one else is being held to the organization's values.
4. Without a stipulation that they are being held to the organizational values, it is difficult to fire high-performing toxic people.

---

effectively the employees are achieving the organization's values. Is anyone going to argue with you holding everyone accountable to achieving the organization's values? I doubt it.

> Leaders need to make the organizational values come alive in the performance management process. If the values are so darned important, then hold *everyone* accountable for achieving these—not just toxic people.

THREE POWERFUL PERFORMANCE MANAGEMENT PRACTICES

Table 6.2 identifies the three most powerful performance management practices to effectively deal with not just toxic individuals, but all your employees, as a means of creating an organizational culture where there is alignment to the espoused values.

TABLE 6.2

Three Powerful Performance Management Practices to Align Your Organization's Culture around Its Values

---

The following three factors contribute to making your performance management process more authentic and values-driven.

1. *Accountability*. Hold everyone accountable to your organization's values.
2. *Integration*. Integrate the values into the performance management process.
3. *Discussion*. Discuss these values regularly one-on-one *and* in team meetings.

It is so interesting to me to hear client responses when I relate to them the importance of holding everyone accountable to the organization's values. They respond with an almost resounding, "Well, of course we do!" But do they? I ask this rhetorical question because I have found that many do not even know what their own organization's values are! When I ask, I often get replies like, "Wait a minute, Mitch. I know I have them in a drawer somewhere!" Or, "I remember seeing these the other day in a conference room. Now, where was that conference room?!" I believe you get the point. Awareness first.

What are some of the best ways for *everyone* in an organization to know what the organization's values are? Hint: It is not on a plaque on a wall, nor is it on a business card! Not that these are bad; they're just not as effective as when these values are integrated into the performance management process. While an individual leader may not likely be able to change what is on the structured performance appraisal form, you *can* have performance discussions centered on the values. Table 6.3 demonstrates how to prepare for a discussion that any leader may wish to have with a team

TABLE 6.3

Preparing for a Sample Discussion around the Organization's Values

The following are the focused sections of a good performance management process that considers the organization's values.

1. *Introduction.* "Our organization has five core values that I want all of us to not only understand but integrate into the fabric of what we do every day. I will hold everyone *accountable* for this."
2. *The conversation.* "Therefore, I am going to have each one of us *integrate* one of these values into our work over the next six months. While I hope that you will align with all the values, I am only focusing on one so that you can concentrate your efforts more effectively. Within the next week I'm going to have a 30-minute *discussion* with each of you. To prepare for this meeting, I want each of you to identify one value that you want to work on—in other words, be better at it than you are currently. And I am including myself in this as well."
3. *Implementation.* "Then, over the next six months, I want you to share with me monthly how you are doing on the achievement of this one value you have selected. I will also share my work in this regard. If you are having difficulty or need me as a resource, that's why I'm here. I will also introduce a new practice whereby we will take 10 minutes once a month at our staff meetings for us to *discuss* what we are doing to more effectively achieve our values."
4. *Development.* "As you know, we have a development section on our performance appraisal form. I will document your values work over the next six months on this form. Of course, the development section will also include the work related to the technical aspects of your job. I hope this provides an additional way for us to achieve our organization's values."

around the organization's values. Within Table 6.3, I have italicized core words from the previous Table 6.2: *accountability, integration,* and *discussion,* so that you can readily see the combination of powerful practices with the sample discussion.

As you can see from this process, no one individual is being singled out. It is a proactive process for everyone. It is useful for toxic individuals and non-toxic alike, but this method *does* help leaders deal with one of the defenses of many toxic people: "Why am I being singled out for violating the values and no one else is?" You are now holding everyone accountable for upholding the values. This will help when you have those gritty discussions about the person's negative behaviors—which almost always violate at least one organizational value. Integrating the values into the performance discussion for everyone also helps if you need to fire a person who is consistently violating the organization's values, while also meeting the performance goals of their job. It can otherwise be difficult to fire them.

> Integrating the values into the performance discussion for everyone also helps if you need to fire a person who is consistently violating the organization's values, while also meeting the performance goals of their job. It can otherwise be difficult to fire them.

A PERFORMANCE MANAGEMENT TEMPLATE

There is a limit to what any one individual leader can do related to the organization's performance management system. What a leader *can* do includes:

- Holding everyone accountable for the achievement of the organization's values.
- Having conversations around these values—both one-on-one and in teams.
- Documenting these value achievements in the organization's performance management system.

This is often as far as any one leader goes. There are two additional strategies that tap into the expertise of the human resources department. The first of these is assessing everyone in the organization based on their

TABLE 6.4

Sample Section of a Performance Appraisal Form with Values Integration

In the same way that all employees are rated on their achievement of the criteria related to job performance, all employees will also be rated on their upholding of the organizational values according to the scale. You will see that there are two important sections—quantitative and qualitative. This is called a "mixed-methods" approach that combines numerical measurement with verbal perspectives. Both are important to add integrity and robustness to our organization's performance management process.

Quantitative Items Section:

	Rating Scale		
	Not Achieved	Somewhat Achieved	Highly Achieved
1. Demonstrates respectful behavior in team meetings	1	2	3
2. When having conflict with a team member, tries to resolve this through respectful dialogue	1	2	3
3. At times of disagreement, listens carefully before responding	1	2	3
4. Provides support to various team members before being asked	1	2	3
5. Acknowledges colleagues for a job well done	1	2	3
6. Uses language that one would be proud of in other social contexts	1	2	3
7. Is inclusive of others in conversations, as needed	1	2	3
8. Is a person to whom co-workers gravitate with questions or concerns	1	2	3
9. Provides feedback in constructive, helpful ways	1	2	3
10. Is the kind of person people enjoy being around	1	2	3

Qualitative Items Section:

Please provide some comments that describe this person's achievement of any of these values, as well as when this individual violated these values:

- *Engagement:* Is open to the opinions and ideas of others; includes and invites team members in conversations as appropriate and relevant
- *Making a difference:* Extends himself/herself to help others at work and beyond

(Continued)

TABLE 6.4 (CONTINUED)

Sample Section of a Performance Appraisal Form with Values Integration

- *Civility:* Operates with respect for others; even when in disagreement, uses language that does not shame or does not appear condescending
- *Dignity:* Treats everyone—no matter the position or level—with the same respect that would make one proud if family members or friends experienced this

Specific Comments:

upholding of established values, using the actual performance appraisal form. Recall that in opening this chapter I shared two statistics. One was that only 20 percent of those who have a performance appraisal form have the organizational values identified on this form. Another statistic—of those who have the values on the form, only 5 percent have the values as items on which one is assessed. So, just as in many performance appraisal forms there is a rating scale for items, there should also be inclusion of these items related to the values. Table 6.4 provides a sample section of what this could look like in any organization. Of course, each organization would have to adapt both the values and rating scales to their own organization's template.

THE 70-30 SPLIT PERFORMANCE MODEL

The second human resources strategy is the *70-30 split performance model.* Dr. Elizabeth Holloway and I have successfully introduced the practice into many organizations. Like the previous strategy of creating a new values-based performance management process, this one needs human resources sanction. In this model, approximately 70 percent of the performance assessment is aligned with organizational tasks; 30 percent is aligned with assessment of the values work. Table 6.5 provides examples of what this 70-30 split could look like in an organization.

> In the 70-30 performance split model, approximately 70 percent of the performance assessment is aligned with organizational tasks; 30 percent is aligned with assessment of the values work.

TABLE 6.5

Examples of How Performance Items Could Be Configured with the 70-30 Split Performance Model

---

70% of the task-based items related to:
- *Performance:* Meeting goals
- *Team development:* Understanding team expectations
- *Feedback:* Accepting constructive criticism
- *Career development:* Managing resources associated with one's own career
- *Time management:* Managing priorities
- *Leadership style:* Delegating important work to others
- *Leadership development:* Coaching others

30% of the values-based items related to:
- *Engagement:* Open to the ideas of others
- *Making a difference:* Volunteering to a cause beyond our work environment
- *Civility:* Operates with respect, using language that is affirming and not having to prove you are right
- *Dignity:* Engages others with the same fairness—no matter the level or position

---

While Table 6.5 is simply a prototype of how one could engage the 70-30 split, I have discovered that it is not important to rigidly adhere to this exact percentage. What *is* important is that a team of human resources professionals and other key leaders determine how to split the task-based and values-based items. The significance of this team effort is to design a template that works for *your* organization—one that addresses both task-based and values-based perspectives. What is critical here is for this team to understand that this serves two purposes. First, it engages everyone in integrating the values into the fabric of what people should be doing every day. Second, it provides a way to cue everyone that they are being assessed on these values, thus not allowing uncivil people to get away with bad behavior. The values work becomes everyone's responsibility and no person can say that she/he is being held to a different standard from everyone else.

PROTOCOL FOR FIRING THE TOXIC PERSON

In some unfortunate circumstances, the toxic person needs to be fired. This occurs when all the best strategies simply have not worked, and the person's presence is detrimental to immediate progress within a team or larger organization. The one strategy that will be of most support in this process is if you, as the leader, have done your due diligent work in integrating the values into your performance management system. What will be of further support is if you have managed the person's performance using both task-based and values-based perspectives. So, even when faced with very high achievers who are uncivil persons, if you have done an outstanding job of documenting, discussing, and evaluating their performances based on these two perspectives of the 70 task-30 values split, you will be in good stead.

> Even with very high achievers who are uncivil persons, if you have done an outstanding job of documenting, discussing, and evaluating their performances based on these two perspectives of the 70 task-30 values split, you will be in good stead.

Ultimately, you do not want to be in a situation where a person tells you, "My performance is superior. I sometimes have to violate the organization's values to achieve this high level of performance. And I am the only one who seems to be held accountable for achieving these values!" A values-based performance process will reduce the probability of this occurring, provide a fair and equitable system to assess values, and deal with toxic people in an effective way. Table 6.6 identifies some of the ways to respond to toxic individuals who claim they sometimes have to violate the organizational values to achieve the business's success.

Some of my clients have asked me why is it so difficult to fire a toxic person? In fact, many have noted it can be even more difficult than someone with poor performance. There are several reasons for this.

TABLE 6.6

Ways in Which You Can Respond to Toxic Individuals Who Say That Sometimes They Have to Violate the Organization's Values

These quotes will provide both content and context in how to deliver the message when organizational values are violated. I suggest you not stick to these overly rigidly but rather, you encapsulate these quotes into your own language and context.
- "We do not achieve our business success by violating organizational values. Therefore, I expect these same values apply to you."
- "I hold all members of my team accountable for helping achieve our organizational values. This includes you without any exception."
- "I need to know if you intend to stop violating the organizational values. If I do not have this commitment from you, we will need to proceed to the next step—a verbal warning (or whatever your human resource practice dictates)."

TABLE 6.7

Why It Is Difficult to Fire a Toxic Person

- They can be clever chameleons, capable of "knocking down and kissing up."
- They have not been held accountable to the organizational values they have violated.
- They are sometimes your highest performers.
- They inspire fear in many—including possibly you as their boss!

First, if you will recall that some toxic people are clever chameleons—very capable of "knocking down and kissing up." Therefore, they escape the detection of the leader who will do the firing. A second reason is related to the organizational values. As I discussed earlier in this chapter, leaders sometimes do not hold toxic employees accountable to living out the values. I see this manifested in many organization's performance management systems, where the values go by the wayside by not being effectively measured. And when accountability to the values arises, it is sometimes too late because these have not been discussed in the context of performance. As well, leaders need to hold everyone accountable to the organization's values—not just the toxic person. A third reason is that many toxic individuals are high performers. Who wants to upset things by confronting high performers? You do, because as you have discovered in this book, the short-term gains by keeping them are nothing compared to the long-term losses to an organization's bottom line and team performance. Table 6.7 summarizes why it is so difficult to fire a toxic person.

7

A Powerful Team Assessment Method

Just as individuals can be toxic protectors and buffers, so can teams. It is a little trickier for teams to identify how they have been protecting and buffering toxic people because of the mix of personalities within teams. Therefore, a more direct assessment method is needed to "peel the onion" of the enabling roles that teams can play. This chapter presents an assessment instrument and method that leaders may use to both assess and build better teams—one that catalyzes the importance of a facilitated discussion of the strengths and improvement areas for the team. The instrument itself does not directly cull out any toxic individual; rather, it identifies how the team members perceive the team performance and dynamics, including those related to toxic behaviors. The discussions in association with the data from this instrument will likely open up a way to address toxic behaviors directly and clearly.

> Just as individuals can be toxic protectors and buffers, so can teams. It is a little trickier for teams to identify how they have been protecting and buffering toxic people because of the mix of personalities within teams. Therefore, a more direct assessment method is needed to "peel the onion" of the enabling roles that teams can play.

The instrument is called the *Campbell-Hallam Team Development Survey*™ (TDS) (Campbell & Hallam, 1994). I would like to begin this discussion with a disclaimer that I have no financial or vested interest in this instrument; it is simply an instrument that I purchase from General Dynamics Information Technology (the vendor) when there is indication from clients that there is need for a team assessment. The TDS is an assessment tool I have used hundreds of times with many organizational clients with great success. In this assessment method, team members evaluate the team on 18 key dimensions related to best practices with associated team effectiveness. The unique aspect of this instrument is that not only team members, but also individuals who are *not* part of the team assess the team on these same 18 dimensions in an anonymous way. These non-team members who work with the team are called "observers" on the instrument. This gives the TDS a special feature that is similar, to some extent, to 360-degree leadership assessment surveys. In the TDS, there is this same 360-degree component in which others who regularly interact with the team, but are not part of the team, provide valuable feedback to the team. Another unique feature that this instrument has is that the team is compared with other teams throughout the United States who have taken the instrument. Therefore, the team sees precisely where it stands on each of these 18 dimensions in comparison with the national average.

In my experiences using this instrument, it provides a forum for team members to take a risk and address the person's behavior in a safe venue. The data simply act as a catalyst to spur on valuable discussion. A rich discussion of areas of strength, challenges, and opportunities—based on the team results—provides a winning combination. Figure 7.1 shows the summary page from a sample team who has gone through this assessment process. In this summary page, the five shaded areas indicate the normed range of scores from a national sample of teams: very low, low, mid-range, high, and very high. The highest team scores are identified by open-diamond marks, team average scores by colored-in squares, and lowest team scores by colored-diamond marks. You can then see how the team scored compared to the national sample on 18 dimensions of team effectiveness.

In Figure 7.2, I selected two pages of several pages in the final report that show what a more detailed report looks like in the TDS. Here, you will see how the team scored itself on each of the items within a specific category. In addition, you will see how the observers rated the team in each category. Since the purpose of sharing these results is to present an overview of the instrument and not be overly focused on specific items, some items have been deleted.

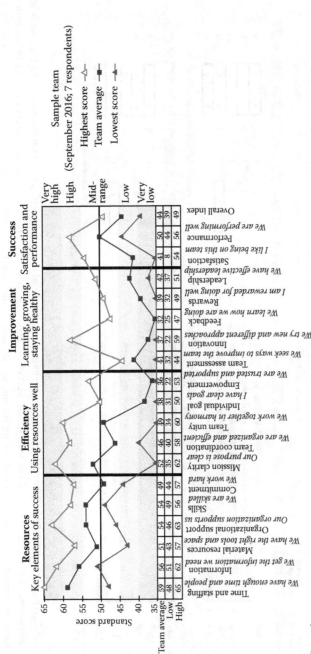

FIGURE 7.1

Campbell-Hallam Team Development Survey™ summary report. This is a sample page from a TDS report that is generated based on data retrieved from two groups: the actual team members as well as those individuals who are not part of the team but have had opportunities to observe the team in action. Scores are plotted in terms of the team's responses to 18 items as well as how the team compares to a normed sample group.

TDS Results for sample team (September 2016; 7 respondents)

Team assessment

	Strongly disagree	Disagree	Slightly disagree	Slightly agree	Agree	Strongly agree	Percent favorable
4.	1	1	5	0	0	0	0
58. We have recently discussed what we did right or wrong on a particular project or job	0	3	4	0	0	0	0
33.	0	0	1	5	1	0	0
Observer item 18.	0	3	1	0	0	0	0

Very high 0
High 0
Mid-range 0
Low 5
Very low 2

Ways to help: Set aside a regular time (e.g., after each major deadline) for discussing what the team is doing well and how it can improve.

Innovation

	Strongly disagree	Disagree	Slightly disagree	Slightly agree	Agree	Strongly agree	Percent favorable
23.	1	3	2	1	0	0	0
36. Our team has a reputation for being innovative	1	2	3	0	2	0	29
48.	0	1	1	1	2	1	43
61.	1	1	0	2	3	0	29
Observer item 17. The team is innovative	0	1	2	0	0	0	0

Very high 0
High 1
Mid-range 0
Low 2
Very low 4

Ways to help:

Feedback

	Strongly disagree	Disagree	Slightly disagree	Slightly agree	Agree	Strongly agree	Percent favorable
30.	0	2	1	0	0	0	0
54.	3	3	1	0	0	0	0
67. The team leader gives members valuable feedback to help them improve	3	2	0	1	1	0	14
11. I am never sure how well I am performing on this team	0	0	1	2	1	3	0
Observer item 20.	0	0	0	3	1	0	25

Very high 0
High 0
Mid-range 1
Low 0
Very low 6

Ways to help: Ask key people (e.g., your customers or teammates) for their honest feedback.

FIGURE 7.2

Two of six detailed pages from the TDS Report. These two sample pages of a completed report (pages 92 and 93 here) demonstrate the team's scores in selected categories, as well as how individuals who are not part of the team (the "observer") rate the team's effectiveness. Six of 18 categories are indicated: team assessment, innovation, feedback, commitment, mission clarity, and team coordination.

(Continued)

TDS results for sample team (September 2016; 7 respondents)

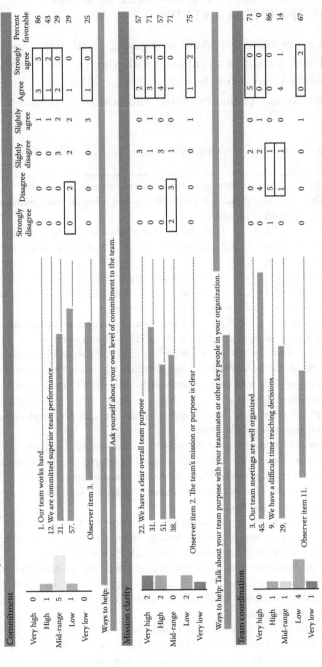

		Strongly disagree	Disagree	Slightly disagree	Slightly agree	Agree	Strongly agree	Percent favorable
Commitment								
	1. Our team works hard.	0	0	0	1	3	3	86
	12. We are committed superior team performance	0	0	1	1	1	2	43
	21.	0	0	3	2	2	0	29
	57.	0	2	2	2	1	0	29
	Observer item 3.	0	0	0	3	1	0	25

Ways to help: Ask yourself about your own level of commitment to the team.

		Strongly disagree	Disagree	Slightly disagree	Slightly agree	Agree	Strongly agree	Percent favorable
Mission clarity								
	22. We have a clear overall team purpose	0	0	3	0	2	2	57
	31.	0	0	1	1	3	2	71
	51.	0	0	3	0	4	0	57
	38.	2	3	1	0	1	0	71
	Observer item 2. The team's mission or purpose is clear	0	0	0	1	1	2	75

Ways to help: Talk about your team purpose with your teammates or other key people in your organization.

		Strongly disagree	Disagree	Slightly disagree	Slightly agree	Agree	Strongly agree	Percent favorable
Team coordination								
	3. Our team meetings are well organized.	0	0	2	0	5	0	71
	45.	0	4	2	1	0	0	0
	9. We have a difficult time reaching decisions.	1	5	1	0	4	1	86
	29.	0	1	1	0	4	1	14
	Observer item 11.	0	0	0	1	0	2	67

Ways to help: Set a goal for regular team planning and organizing (e.g., meet briefly each Monday to discuss the week ahead).

FIGURE 7.2 (CONTINUED)

Two of six detailed pages from the TDS Report. These two sample pages of a completed report (pages 92 and 93 here) demonstrate the team's scores in selected categories, as well as how individuals who are not part of the team (the "observer") rate the team's effectiveness. Six of 18 categories are indicated: team assessment, innovation, feedback, commitment, mission clarity, and team coordination.

CASE SIMULATION OF THE CAMPBELL-HALLAM TEAM DEVELOPMENT SURVEY™

To get a feel for how this instrument is engaged, I will share how the process played itself out with a recent team with whom I have consulted. Table 7.1 provides a template of the tool, and what follows is a description of the team dynamics that occurred and how these helped team

TABLE 7.1

Summary of What a Sample Team Experiences Using the Campbell-Hallam Team Development Survey™ (TDS)

The following categories indicate the various phases I have engaged to help teams understand the TDS. I have found that this kind of discussion is key for team members to understand the value of this instrument.

1. *Initial meeting with the leader.* The facilitator meets with the leader of the team to discuss the purpose of the TDS and set dates for both the TDS distribution and the team development session.

2. *Introduction of the TDS process to the team.* Facilitator convenes the entire team, discusses the purpose of the TDS, and shares a sample team report from other teams outside the organization without names to protect anonymity.

3. *Team discussion regarding the TDS process.* The team asks questions of the facilitator in order to gain a better sense of the purpose of the TDS with this team.

4. *Selection of external observers who rate the team.* The team discusses and identifies whom they would like as the observers (those individuals who are not members of the team but work regularly with the team and can provide a wider view of what it is like to work with this team).

5. *Electronic completion of the TDS.* The TDS is sent out electronically for completion by both the team members and observers.

6. *Report generation and distribution.* A summary report is sent to the facilitator, who distributes either hard copies or electronic copies depending upon the client's preference.

7. *Team engagement in action planning.* The facilitator reviews the entire TDS report with the team, and engages the team in a discussion of strengths, areas for improvement, and action planning.

8. *Engagement with observers.* It is important that the team determine how to engage the observers. This can range from simply sharing selected written results with the observers to involving them in a conversation of what the team has learned, to full-blown engagement of some observers in the action planning (with their willingness, of course).

9. *One-month follow-up with the team.* One month following the team development session, the facilitator meets with the team and coaches them further regarding obstacles and future direction.

10. *Three months follow-up with the team.* Three months following the team development session, the facilitator engages in more follow-up team coaching, addresses any potential challenges, and helps them measure results.

members understand their roles in contributing to a toxic individual's behavior—and what they did about it. Please note that I have changed some of the contexts of the situation to protect confidentiality and anonymity. These alterations did not compromise the content or intent of the case.

The sample team I have selected for purposes of demonstrating this instrument is a marketing team in the airline industry. I was called in by the Vice President of Human Resources to help improve a situation where there was a lack of trust with a team member whom the team viewed as highly toxic. After discussing the situation with the VP, I proposed an initial meeting with the leader who concurred with the situation but did not know how to handle this. I stated that the next step should be a team session in which I would explore the opinions of the entire team—members and leaders—to gauge initial thoughts.

Once I received the leader's approval to proceed, I met with the entire team to introduce them to the overall TDS process as a way to collect "hard data" on the critical needs of the team; they all concurred that improvement was needed but no one volunteered that it might relate to a toxic team member. Instead, everyone was vague about the issue. I shared what a sample report looks like, so they would have a sense of what to expect when they received one, and to help them understand the purpose of the instrument, mainly how it could be used to help the team put a stake in the ground in order to resolve the problem. At this stage, they reviewed the analyzed data and how they might interpret the report if this were their team. A rich discussion occurred regarding how confidential the information was, how they could use this kind of information to build their own team, and my perspectives on how other teams experienced this process. Once I shared information with them that assured them of the importance and confidentiality of this process, they were ready to proceed.

Some of the most interesting conversation with this team—and literally *all* teams I have engaged in this process—is a discussion on who should be the observers. The discussion included whether they should select external raters who would give them glowing reviews, or those who had extensive longevity with the team; the discussion even included not having any external raters because no one knew the complexity and demands of their jobs. What is fascinating is that this is the kind of discussion that goes on

100 percent of the time when I introduce the concept of team observers. Ultimately, here's what this team decided:

- The observers were those who would provide honest feedback—positive and negative.
- These external raters would range in years of experience with the team from one year to 15 years.
- The observers were those who had extensive interaction with the team, such that they were considered either "partners" or "internal customers" of the team.
- The leader of the team would meet with the external raters to share with them that they had been selected for this important role, and asked if they would be willing to do this. If so, the leader would then share with the observers that they would receive formal instructions for completing the evaluation electronically within a few days.

Once the data had been analyzed from both the team members and observers—and sent to me for final distribution to the team members—I then began mapping out a plan for proceeding with the team. For example, I noted any obstacles or challenges anticipated—including reluctant team members—and how to help the team arrive at agreed-upon target goals based on the data. During the session, we discussed how to share what they had learned from the external observers. At the end of the session, the combined data from these observers and their own internal team helped them move to a proactive course of action. Some of the actions they incorporated into a three-month plan included:

- The individual who was regarded as "disruptive and uncivil" (because the term "toxic" is not facilitative in this context) understood how some of her condescending and shaming remarks were not useful for team performance.
- She volunteered to work with a coach to learn how to: extinguish condescending feedback to team members; provide corrective and reinforcing feedback on a consistent and positive basis; stop shaming individuals one-on-one and in public venues.
- The team defined "shaming" and "condescending" behaviors in concrete, specific language, with rich examples.
- Beyond the individual, the TDS process helped the team develop an improved service delivery model with three of their key internal customers (who were also part of the observer group).

- The team further generated an internal process for sharing critical client data with all team members and designed a team-generated matrix that would compare best-in-class benchmarks with team data from key customers.
- The team scheduled three team-building sessions for the entire team focused on improving the top four areas (identified through the TDS) of most significant concern among the team.

After six months of working with the team on these core actions, I conducted individual interviews with each of the team members with the following results:

- The toxic individual significantly reduced her shaming and condescending behaviors such that team members reported greater trust and confidence in the leader.
- Through an internally generated customer survey, key clients reported that the team improved their responsiveness to client issues, resolved problems more quickly, and helped them build their business so that they could serve their external customers more effectively.
- Customers further reported that the team had improved on four out of five best-in-class benchmarks associated with team performance.
- Service delivery with clients improved as demonstrated by results in follow-up focus groups and surveys.

In the case of another team from the healthcare industry, for whom Dr. Elizabeth Holloway and I facilitated the TDS, one of their tangible outcomes was the design of a process for integrating the organization's values into the team culture. Table 7.2 demonstrates this method. For one nursing team who went through the TDS, something clicked about what they could do to impact the organizational values. They developed a makeshift matrix that they placed on the dry-erase board in the nursing station. The first column of this matrix identified how some of the things they say to patients, while not necessarily wrong, are not conducive to valuing the patient. So, for example, instead of just "rooming" the patient to an exam room, they thought that using the term "escort" would be much more valued by the patient. And you can see how it relates to the importance of a culture change in the third column. In similar fashion,

TABLE 7.2

How One Team Developed a Team Culture Process as a Result of the TDS Assessment

Building a respectful team to impact performance		
What we used to do or say:	What we do or say now:	Why change?
"We room the patient."	"We escort the patient."	This ties in to our organizational values of respect and patient service.
"I'll get you a cup of coffee and blanket (for chemo patient), but may not be around to do it later."	"I'll get you a cup of coffee and blanket and will show your partner where these are kept, should I not be around later."	This demonstrates how we value the nurse-patient encounter and ultimately impacts the outcome for the patient—both emotionally and physically.

when a patient (who is coming to this clinic because of a serious illness) asks for a cup of coffee and blanket, the typical response in column one is essentially a "yes... but." Instead, you will see the more affirming response in column two, with the rationale for the change in column three. With this example, while it did not identify toxic behaviors per se, something interesting occurred in this regard. The toxic member of the team saw his behavior loud and clear, realizing that he needed to change. It was fascinating that *all* the team members saw how they could change as well in a more civil direction!

One more interesting development occurred with this team. The makeshift matrix spread like wildfire throughout the organization—so much so that other teams starting adapting this same method of culture change! And just as interesting, this matrix was featured in the company newsletter and ultimately became a permanent "fixture" in the organization for team culture change. As well, it became an introductory method during new employee orientation to demonstrate how this medical facility impacts patient service through its team culture. And with this model, the nursing team, as well as other teams, continually update the matrix to make it adaptable to its current concerns.

WHAT HAPPENS WHEN THE TEAM LEADER IS TOXIC

I recently facilitated a team where it was the *leader* who was the toxic person. When some of the results from the TDS indicated that the team lacked "empowerment, feedback, and support" from the leader, and that team satisfaction was low, the leader was shocked. In facilitating the discussion, I shared with the leader that there were clear items of strength: the team perceived that the leader was highly skilled, had a clear vision, and believed in the team's mission. The leader seemed relieved to be reminded of this, but heavy work was still needed to tackle the discussion around the areas of her leadership deficits. The data supported the consensus of the group on the toxicity of the leader.

> I recently facilitated a team where it was the *leader* who was the toxic person. When some of the items indicated that the team lacked "empowerment, feedback, and support" from the leader, and that team satisfaction was low, the leader was shocked.

Rather than label the leader with negative words, I asked the team to describe the behavior in concrete and specific terms—along with examples. Here's what they identified as the top leadership behaviors needing improvement. First, they focused on how the boss engaged in condescending remarks at team meetings (e.g., telling team members that their work was not up to par without concrete explanation; relating that someone is "absolutely" wrong without letting the team member explain; telling the team that the leader has seen better teams in grade school). Second, they described the boss's shaming of team members one-on-one and in public (e.g., calling someone "unskilled" in front of others; grabbing a report from a team member and saying that she will give this to someone who has "some brains" to complete it).

Obviously, this was a most difficult conversation beginning with the fact that the leader was not aware of her "toxic" behaviors. She *eventually* thanked the group for bringing these to her attention and asked the group why they never said anything to her about this. After trying several times to give her feedback, which failed, the team members had different ways of dealing with the situation. Some said they just spent less time at work and more time working from home (corroborating the statistic from Chapter 2 that documented that 22% of targets of incivility were less committed to the organization and spent less time at work) (Pearson & Porath, 2009). Others said they came to her support and tried to persuade others that in spite of these behaviors, she was highly productive and led a high-achieving team (toxic protectors). Some actually said that they would quit (aligning with the statistic noted in Chapter 2 that 51% reported that they were highly likely to quit) (Kusy & Holloway, 2009). There were those who said they gossiped about the leader, taking particular "joy" out of seeing her dig her heels into the quagmire further (also known as "secondary gain"). And finally, others reported that those who were "favorites" asked for additional responsibilities so that those who were not her "favorites" wouldn't have to interact as much with the leader (toxic buffering).

The rich discussion that the TDS catalyzed was the fact that toxic protecting and toxic buffering allowed the problem to continue without leader awareness. The leader did disagree with the fact that the "shaming" remarks were not meant to be shaming but rather meant to inspire to better performance. The team came down on her regarding this because it didn't matter the intent; it was still shaming. The team determined that what was needed was to avoid the label, and simply wanted these behaviors stopped. What was most revealing was the fact that this leader eventually labeled herself as "not respectful" and apologized to the team.

An action plan was set up between the team and the leader. The leader said that not only would she curtail her "disrespectful" behaviors but gave permission for the team to identify when she engages in these behaviors; she asked that team members do this privately. If uncivil behaviors occur, team members can proactively pull the leader aside and give feedback by describing the behavior and the impact this behavior has had on the individual and/or the team.

What is most fascinating about this process is that the leader did not "believe" these behaviors until she saw two important dimensions of this instrument. One is the way in which the team experiences were corroborated by the observers. Hence, the importance of this 360-team process that the TDS catalyzes! The other is that the data from the team were normed on teams across the United States, so that this team (including the leader) could see how they scored in relationship to these national teams. The team (including the leader) acknowledged that they would not have come to these action strategies and would not have had the "guts" to push forward had they not had this instrument.

> The rich discussion that the TDS catalyzed was the fact that toxic protecting and toxic buffering allowed the problem to continue without leader awareness.

Please note that the importance of the process that I have unfolded here is not necessarily the result of *this* assessment tool. The TDS is simply an assessment tool for which I have both great respect and familiarity. *Any* assessment tool that assesses team performance in an unbiased and systematic way will likely help unclog team minds with respect to performance and behaviors. With any assessment system, one never knows what will be uncovered. This is one of the reasons that I believe that the facilitator must be prepared to take the team where the data *and* the team indicate. Your human resources professional could be an excellent choice in this regard—to either facilitate or recommend facilitators in your area.

HOW TO BEST ENGAGE THE CAMPBELL-HALLAM TEAM DEVELOPMENT SURVEY™

There are many reasons to want to use a team assessment instrument such as the Campbell-Hallam Team Development Survey™. There is no one rationale for its use. As stated previously, it has not been designed to bring to the surface a toxic individual. It has been designed to have team members consider how their actions impact team performance. Table 7.3 delineates some of the reasons to consider using a team assessment instrument such as the Campbell-Hallam Team Development Survey™.

TABLE 7.3

Reasons for Using a Team Assessment Tool

- The team wishes to assess its strengths and areas for improvement.
- Team performance does not meet expectations.
- The team has been getting feedback from those outside the team that there are performance concerns.
- The team leader has concerns regarding the team's effectiveness.

DIFFERENCES BETWEEN THE CAMPBELL-HALLAM TEAM DEVELOPMENT SURVEY™ AND TRADITIONAL CULTURE ASSESSMENT TOOLS

Often leaders have told me that they have used a team assessment survey in which external team members have provided feedback about the team. When I questioned these leaders further, I discovered that they indeed did *not* use an instrument in which individuals external to the team provided feedback. Instead, what I learned was that what these leaders were referring to was a much more traditional culture assessment survey where an organization was assessed in total—but not a team. Table 7.4 identifies the distinctions between the Campbell-Hallam Team Development Survey™ and more traditional culture assessment surveys.

I hope you are able to see the value in an instrument such as the Campbell-Hallam Team Development Survey™. In summary, what is important to understand incorporates the following points:

- No one instrument does everything.
- One does not have to use the Campbell-Hallam Team Development Survey™; this is one prototype of how to gather data from internal team members as well as individuals who are outside the team.
- There are critical distinctions between the Campbell-Hallam Team Development Survey™ and more traditional culture assessment surveys.

By following these basic guidelines, you will likely make a more informed decision in how to assess teams to achieve maximum potential, as well as understand how toxic behaviors can erode team performance.

TABLE 7.4

Distinctions Between the Campbell-Hallam Team Development Survey™ and More Traditional Culture Assessment Surveys

Campbell-Hallam TeamDevelopment Survey™	Culture Assessment Surveys
Focused on one team	Usually focused on the organization
People outside team rate one team	No external raters of one team
Internal team members rate the team	Organization members rate organization
Facilitator external to team is critical	External facilitator not critical

8

Remain Vigilant

I begin this chapter with a question. When you have individual meetings with your direct reports, what's the agenda for these "one-on-ones"? Here's my guess based on my years of experience coaching leaders and leading teams in organizations. You probably address such things as your direct report's current projects, how her team is doing, how various projects fit into the wider organizational strategic plan, and identification of those employees who are "stars" as well as those who present specific performance challenges. However, these one-on-one meetings do not often address toxic behavior because many times the leader may not be aware of these behaviors because of the "knock down and kiss up" action. This chapter provides a method to discern these behaviors, along with a process for doing something about it.

ARE YOUR ONE-ON-ONE MEETINGS REALLY ENOUGH?

In working with direct reports, effective leaders serve as coaches for short-term, performance-based projects as well as mentors for longer-term, relationship-oriented development. However, even in the best of coaching and mentoring, leaders may get biased views if all they gather is the information the direct reports present. While 360-degree feedback systems provide a diverse range of anonymous survey data from the views of many around the leader—including direct reports and peers, as well as non-anonymous data from the boss—it is often not enough. What's missing? Dialogue with those reporting to your direct reports! Enter the practice of *skip-level discussions*.

While 360-degree feedback systems provide a diverse range of anonymous survey data from the views of many around the leader—including direct reports and peers, as well as non-anonymous data from the boss—it is often not enough. What's missing? Dialogue with those reporting to your direct reports! Enter the practice of *skip-level discussions*.

SKIP-LEVEL DISCUSSIONS

Years ago I engaged a mantra that I believe synthesizes the essence of the skip-level discussion. *Everyone has the right and responsibility of good leadership. If you are getting it, tell others. If you are not, tell the right people.* To live up to this mantra, I have found that the skip-level discussion is an effective practice. The skip-level discussion helps leaders remain vigilant about their team domain through a process of regularly scheduled and ad hoc conversations with those who are two levels down from them on the organizational chart. The express purpose here is for leaders to really understand what is going on in their area from not only those reporting to them but those who are two levels away—those who report to those who report to them. One-on-ones with direct reports are simply not enough. These one-on-ones, while needed, can present unbiased views because they are between a leader and the direct report only. Table 8.1 provides a description of the primary components needed in good skip-level discussions.

Everyone has the right and responsibility of good leadership. If you are getting it, tell others. If you are not, tell the right people. To live up to this mantra, I have found that the skip-level discussion is an effective practice.

In getting a feel for the skip-level discussion, it is important to keep in mind a basic tenet of human behavior: when trying to improve human behavior, no one strategy is foolproof. I mention this with respect to the skip-level discussion because there is often pushback from both leaders *and* direct reports. "What if I get fired for opening my mouth to my boss's boss? What if my direct report says something to my boss that I am not aware of?" My response to these and many other questions that emanate due to the anxiety of this practice is: Is it better to say nothing? Or is it better to get these issues out in the open? There are no easy answers here. I have found that if the practice is designed with integrity, along with as

TABLE 8.1

Components of the Skip-Level Discussion

1. *Introduce the practice of the skip-level discussion.* The leader announces to everyone in her entire span of control that she will be introducing a new practice called the "skip-level discussion."

2. *State the purpose.* The leader shares that the purpose of this is to better understand the leadership strengths and improvement areas for each person's boss, through conversation.

3. *What it looks like.* Every six months the leader will meet individually with the direct reports of the person normally reporting to her. At this time, the leader will ask if each person is getting the kind of leadership they need. What are the leadership strengths of their boss? What areas for improvement are needed? Do you have any concerns or special affirmations about your boss you would like to share? In addition to this structured meeting every six months, the leaders invite each person to meet with the boss's boss whenever they have an issue or something positive to report related to the leadership they are receiving.

4. *Isn't this just a way to get even with your boss?* This is the primary question my clients often ask me about this process. Yes, it can be a way to get back at a toxic boss. However, if someone *does* have a toxic boss, then there needs to be structured vehicles for addressing this. And the skip-level discussion further provides guidelines to reduce the probability of doing this just to get even with their boss.

5. *Engage the criteria.* The primary criteria for effective skip-level discussions include:
   • Proactive: In this case, the leader shares with everyone that she will meet with each individual every six months to touch base on areas of strength and areas of need.
   • Reactive: This occurs whenever anyone has a concern about the leadership they are receiving from their boss *or* if someone wants to affirm a particular strength of their boss.

6. *The process is not confidential nor anonymous.* If necessary, the leader may need to follow up on this and investigate further. Just as importantly, if there is a particular issue that someone is having with his boss, you want to get this out in the open so it does not get worse, cause undue anxiety, or in the most severe case—cause someone to quit.

7. *Assure as much protection as possible.* It is important that you assure as much as you are able to the individual that you will do everything possible to reduce any undue retaliation.

8. *Be sure to have a more inclusive follow-up meeting.* Let's assume the worst and that someone is about to quit because of a toxic boss. First, good thing you had this meeting, because you may not have even been aware of this until now. Remember, these people are often able to keep their toxic behavior hidden. Second, you listen and then suggest that you will set up a meeting with the individual, her boss, you, and ideally a human resources professional.

9. *The action plan.* It could be that the boss is a toxic person. It could also be that the direct report has had performance problems and the boss was just doing her job in challenging the individual to better performance. Whatever the reason is, there needs to be an action plan that documents the conversation with a clear plan for proceeding.

10. *Follow-up.* It is important that shortly after this meeting, follow-up occur to assess progress and, if needed, appropriate next steps.

much protection as possible to genuinely create a more positive and effective work environment, then the pros outweigh the cons.

> In getting a feel for the skip-level discussion, it is important to keep in mind a basic tenet of human behavior: when trying to improve human behavior, no one strategy is foolproof.

CASE EXAMPLE OF A SKIP-LEVEL CONVERSATION

To get a real feel for how this process can go, let's consider a typical conversation synthesized from several of my clients who have engaged in this method.

Tom (Person two levels below the boss's boss). "Carol, I'm a little frightened in talking with you about my boss. I believed you when you said there is integrity to the skip-level process and that you will do what you can to improve the situation."

Carol (Boss's boss). "That's right, Tom. I can't guarantee everything will be rosy after our conversation, but what I can guarantee is that I will do everything possible to bring us all together to resolve whatever is troubling you. Let's start by your sharing what's going on."

Tom. "My boss, Pete, belittles me constantly both when I am alone as well as in front of others. If I do not complete projects exactly as he wants, he will tell me such things as: 'I might as well have done this myself'... or 'I thought you could handle this responsibility, but I guess I was wrong'... or 'This report made me look foolish in front of others. You're incompetent and an idiot.'"

Carol. "If this is what was said, I can see how you are troubled by this. Let's take a step back and consider some factors that have led up to this. Tom, I believe there is never a call for demeaning remarks. I want to understand your performance up to this point. Have you been performing as expected?"

Tom. "I had my performance review with Pete three months ago. I brought it along for you to see. I have met expectations in most areas and exceeded expectations in two of these. I can tell you that if this goes on, I may have to consider looking for a position elsewhere in this company or have to leave the company."

Carol. "I hope it doesn't come to that. Have you tried talking with Pete about your concerns?"

Pete. "Yes. I asked him to please stop belittling me alone and in front of others. He said he only does this because he knows I have so much potential. That's a bunch of crap. If I have all this potential, then there are better ways to motivate me."

Carol. Let's see if we can problem-solve this together. And when I say 'together,' I mean with Pete and Sam, our human resources director. I believe that with just the two of us, we will keep going back and forth on intent of the behavior, expectations, and performance factors. It's best to get all the players here, including our human resources liaison who knows so much about behavioral expectations. OK?"

Tom. "I'd rather not. Do I have a choice here? I thought you would resolve this as you said when you announced this program."

Carol. "I believe I had said that I would do everything possible to get an issue resolved—but that I alone would not nor could do everything. In this circumstance, I think the best route is to get everyone involved. Would you still be OK with this?"

Tom. "Could I lose my job over this?"

Carol. "Based on the excellent performance review that I have pulled form your HR file, no. You will not lose your job."

Tom. "OK. I will go along with this because I trust you, Carol."

Carol. "Great, Tom. I will schedule a meeting for some time tomorrow."

(Carol arranges meeting for the next day.)

Carol. "As all of you know, Tom came to speak with me about his concerns regarding the leadership he has been receiving from Pete. First, I want to affirm that Tom did everything according to our skip-level criteria. He tried to resolve this on his own. Since that did not work, he came to me. Second, I know there are many perspectives here and I simply want us to chat about this together. I do not have all the answers. Third, I'd like to start with Tom relating his concerns."

Tom. "This is very difficult for me. I am trusting the process and that nothing negative will happen to me as a result of my being honest and direct here—like losing my job."

Sam (human resources director). "Tom, no one will lose their jobs over this... not you or Pete."

Tom. "I have been trying to meet all your expectations, Pete. I'm afraid I haven't been because your belittling comments one-on-one and in public indicate I have not been performing as expected. For example, with the recent customer merger project, I gave it to you several days before and you told me, 'It's garbage. I might as well have done this myself.' And on the internal branding project, you told me that I didn't meet expectations. Specifically, you had these choice words for me, 'I thought you could handle this responsibility, but I guess I was wrong. This report will make me look foolish in front of others. You're incompetent and an idiot.'"

Sam. "Pete, did you say those things?"

Pete. "Well, sort of. I didn't think I used those kinds of harsh words, but I can't honestly recall. I want Tom to know I am saying these things because I know he is capable of outstanding performance."

Carol. "Let's get things clear here. Our organizational value of respectful engagement does not tolerate any kind of belittling language. 'Idiot' and 'incompetent' are clear examples of belittling language. This must stop."

Pete. "Tom, I am ashamed I used this language and I apologize."

Sam. "Pete, that's a great start but not enough. I would like to explore two areas here. First, setting appropriate expectations. Second, Tom, you need to be very clear if you do not understand these expectations or expectations were not set. So, regarding the first expectation: I want you to sit down with Tom and be very explicit about what you want to see in various assignments from Tom. In fact, identifying these in an email would be a great start along with a conversation about them. To the second point of your needing to clarify, Tom, I want you to be very direct when you do not understand an assignment. Better to do this ahead of time than later. How does this sound to both of you?"

Tom. "Works for me. Sam, I have been reluctant to ask for clarification because of the belittling I might receive. But I will try this again as I haven't done this for quite some time."

Pete. "Also works for me. Good idea regarding spelling out the project criteria clearly ahead of time. And again, I will not belittle any longer. I do want you to know, Tom, that if the assignment is not done according to standards, I will call you on this."

Tom. "That's fine, Pete. I just do not want to be called names."

Carol. "*I would like to add my two cents worth into this conversation. First, I am pleased with how professional and honest Pete and Tom have been. Thank you. Second, I do want to follow up with both of you together in one week and then one month following this. Third, one of the goals I want you to put into your next year's plan, Pete, is to work on providing clear expectations on assignments. Likewise, for you, Tom, I want you to include in your next year's goals that you will seek clarification for any expectations you do not understand or have questions on. I look forward to a positive result from this skip-level discussion.*"

As you can hopefully see from this sample case, the discussion certainly will depend upon the issues presented. The important points to keep the process running smoothly are:

1. Engage key stakeholders.
2. Set clear expectations.
3. Follow-up.
4. Have a conversation where no one person takes over or rambles.

These basic criteria will keep the process genuine and operating with integrity. Please note that the sample provided was for the ad hoc issue that arises. But having regularly scheduled conversations as a more pro-active method is another way to remain vigilant.

COMPARING THE SKIP-LEVEL DISCUSSION WITH 360-DEGREE FEEDBACK

Many leaders have pointed out to me that they do not need this skip-level discussion because they know what's going on through the 360-degree leader feedback process in their organizations. This may be true, as the 360 process is an excellent way to know what is going on in the organization. However, there are two areas where the skip-level discussion is superior.

First, there has been significant abuse of the 360 process. Some of the latest research demonstrates that 360 methods should be primarily for *development*, not a means of performance appraisal—and results should not be tied to compensation. This means that the boss of the individual being assessed does not automatically receive the feedback from his/her direct report. I know this might create a fly in the ointment for the way many organizations engage in 360 feedback. There is significant research that has demonstrated many perils when the boss of the individual going through the 360 process automatically gets the feedback of the individual being assessed. Why? The person being assessed could go to those direct reports and/or peers doing the rating and stress how this is linked to their performance appraisal process—and their pay. Therefore, there could be subtle pressures to get people to rate the individual higher than warranted. Further, when the boss receives the feedback automatically—and others know this—there could be a tendency to inflate ratings when the person assessed is doing a good job, as well as deflate the ratings more than is warranted if the person being assessed is a toxic person.

Here's how I handle 360 methods with my own clients. I make it clear that there should be a conversation between the person being assessed and the boss, but that the boss does not automatically receive this feedback. The person who should be engaged first is an internal or external consultant to help the individual make sense of the data and effectively design a course of action as a result. I further stipulate that many people have taken time to complete the assessment tool and the person being assessed has a responsibility to share what they learned with others, as appropriate and relevant. This would include sharing pertinent information or action plans with their direct reports, peers, and yes, even their boss. This means that if someone has learned that they have been engaging in uncivil behaviors (like shaming others), it is up to the individual being assessed to determine if this is something she would like to share with her boss. If so, then the boss can coach or engage others as appropriate.

> Some of the latest research demonstrates that 360 methods should be primarily for *development*, not a means of performance appraisal. This means that the boss of the individual being assessed does not automatically receive the feedback from his/her direct report—and results should not be tied to compensation.

The second way that the skip-level is different from the 360 process is that a discussion is mandated in the skip-level, but not in the 360 process. While a discussion is certainly encouraged in the 360 method, it is up to each individual being assessed as to whether they wish to discuss

TABLE 8.2

Distinctions and Similarities Between the Skip-Level Process and the 360-Degree Feedback Method

Many clients often misinterpret the skip-level process as the same as the 360-feedback process. The following compares the two and helps leaders make an informed decision of whether to use one or the other, or both.

Skip-Level	360-Feedback
Not anonymous	Anonymous
Confidential	Confidential
Informal	Formal
Discussion mandated	Discussion highly recommended
No formal instrument	Formal instrument
Human resources should be consulted	Human resources should be consulted
No consultant needed	Consultant recommended (internal or external)

their results with others. Table 8.2 provides some of the distinctions and similarities between the skip-level process and the 360-degree feedback method.

I have found that a combination of the skip-level and 360-degree feedback is ideal. The primary benefit of the skip-level is the required conversation; the main benefit of the 360 is the multiple assessors providing a rich mix of perspectives. When both methods are activated in an organization, the organization will experience more goal-oriented leadership behaviors as well as more relationship-oriented, respectful behaviors. And this is what we want in leadership today—enhanced goal achievement with respectful engagement. And in tandem, these two methods are superb ways for leaders to remain vigilant and deal directly and swiftly with toxic behaviors.

9

How to Build a Culture
of Everyday Civility

This final chapter of *Why I Don't Work Here Anymore* positions everyday civility (Kusy & Holloway, 2014) as a practice to which all organizations need to aspire. In Chapters 1 and 2, I presented a business case for doing this. In the remaining chapters, I presented the operational cases for how this gets done. Synthesizing business and operational cases into a final chapter brings me to this conclusion. "It takes a village," so they say, to create a culture where toxic individuals do not get away with bad behavior. In this final chapter, I help leaders understand the steps needed for instilling a culture of everyday civility defined as a norm of respect that is modeled, reinforced, and integrated into the daily culture of the organization (Kusy & Holloway, 2014). What can leaders do to "walk the talk"? How do they integrate everyday civility values into daily conversations? These questions have been addressed in this book through evidence-based practices—demonstrated to show results. With this final chapter, I summarize these practices into a cohesive plan of action.

THE PROBLEM, THE ACTION, AND THE EXPECTED OUTCOME

Let's face it, doing something about any problem we experience takes focus and commitment. Because toxic people exhaust so much of our emotions and financial resources, sometimes we just want to hide and hope the problem will go away on its own. As you have read in *Why I Don't Work Here Anymore*, it takes a systems approach to understand and intervene.

TABLE 9.1

The Problem-Action-Outcome Matrix

Begin engaging this matrix by reflecting on the specific problem related to toxic behavior that is having an impact on you, team member(s), and/or the organization. Write all the issues that come to mind and place these in the "problem" column. Then, review the 18 core actions we have discussed in this book and see which one(s) of these might be useful in addressing the problem. Finally, identify the expected outcomes you hope to achieve with action(s). To assist you in recalling each of the actions, here is a list of the primary ones and the chapters in which these action were discussed:

1. The 4-step apology   (Chapter 1)
2. Impact of toxic people assessed with   (Chapter 2)
   the financial template
3. Explanation of the myths about toxic   (Chapter 2)
   people
4. Cost-benefit strategy on whether to   (Chapter 3)
   give feedback
5. Direct-report feedback strategy   (Chapter 3)
6. Peer feedback strategy   (Chapter 3)
7. Boss feedback strategy   (Chapter 3)
8. Feedback conversation starters   (Chapter 3)
9. Disengagement of toxic protectors   (Chapter 4)
10. Disengagement of toxic buffers   (Chapter 4)
11. New recruiting practices that engage   (Chapter 5)
    others
12. Non-hypothetical hiring questions   (Chapter 5)
13. New practices for exit interviews   (Chapter 5)
14. Values integration into performance   (Chapter 6)
    discussions
15. 70-30 task-values performance split   (Chapter 6)
16. Campbell-Hallam Team Development   (Chapter 7)
    Survey™
17. Skip-level discussions   (Chapter 8)
18. New ways to use 360 feedback   (Chapter 8)

Problem	**Potential Action(s)**	**Expected Outcome(s)**
Identify the problem in terms of its impact on you, the team, and/or organization.	List potential actions to each problem?	What outcomes do you expect impacting each problem?

Problem 1:

Problem 2:

Problem 3:

To assist your initiating actions with the most successful outcomes, I have created a problem-action-outcome matrix (Table 9.1). This will provide an overview of the "lay of the land" so that you may best apply a systems approach to doing something about your negative situation.

PRIORITIZING YOUR ACTIONS

Now that you have the matrix completed, action needs to begin. Unfortunately, this can appear quite daunting if the problem has persisted for some time and little has been done. So, "Where do I start?" is a key question. I suggest dividing your potential actions into those that are easy to implement, as well as those more difficult to implement.

Table 9.2 provides a checklist that identifies all the actions discussed in this book in one comprehensive location. This also serves as a cue sheet that will help remind you in an abbreviated way the various actions you may plan to take. This checklist has a second benefit: it provides a simple way to briefly share with others various strategies. One leader with whom I worked had it on her desk and used it to introduce talking points during her one-on-one meetings.

As you may envision, using this cue sheet can become a very tailor-made process in which leaders discern those areas that create the most value for them and their organizations. And sharing this instrument with others can become fuel for wonderful talking points regarding everyday civility— a concept and practice whose time has come!

For example, for potential actions in the "easy and high impact" category, a leader may determine that the easiest way to introduce the importance of everyday civility is to tell everyone that she has taken one of the quizzes in this book to better understand uncivil behaviors and determine if she is an uncivil person. And as a second step, the leader may encourage everyone to take this same quiz; this leaves the door open for talking about this further with her. And as a third step, she can share with others what she learned about her own disruptive behaviors and what she intends to do differently.

For actions that are difficult to implement but still have a high payoff, one of the cautions I share with leaders at this stage is that these actions could be too difficult for any one leader, thus making it easy to decide to do nothing. I suggest breaking down the actions into more manageable "chunks."

TABLE 9.2

Checklist of Top Actions for Dealing with Toxic Behaviors

To determine the top actions you may want to take to begin establishing a culture of everyday civility in your organization, please review the results from Table 9.1. Color in the category that most identifies with the action(s) from Table 9.1.

Then determine if these action(s) are easy and high impact or difficult and high impact.

	Easy and High Impact	Difficult and High Impact	Chapter
1. The 4-step apology.	O	O	1
2. Impact of toxic people assessed with the financial template.	O	O	2
3. Explanation of the myths about toxic people.	O	O	2
4. Cost-benefit strategy on whether to give feedback.	O	O	3
5. Direct-report feedback strategy.	O	O	3
6. Peer feedback strategy.	O	O	3
7. Boss feedback strategy.	O	O	3
8. Feedback conversation starters.	O	O	3
9. Disengagement of toxic protectors.	O	O	4
10. Disengagement of toxic buffers.	O	O	4
11. New recruiting practices that engage others.	O	O	5
12. Non-hypothetical hiring questions.	O	O	5
13. New practices for exit interviews.	O	O	5
14. Values integration into performance discussions.	O	O	6
15. 70-30 task-values performance split.	O	O	6
16. Campbell-Hallam Team Development Survey™.	O	O	7
17. Skip-level discussions.	O	O	8
18. New ways to use 360 feedback.	O	O	8

Instructions for interpreting results:

1. First, consider those areas in the "easy and high impact" category. Any of the items here would be a great beginning point.
2. Second, consider those in the "difficult and high impact" category. You may either choose to break these down into more manageable goals or seek someone to help you with this item, as appropriate and relevant.
3. Third, if appropriate, feel free to check out your strategies with someone who knows you well and could provide honest feedback and support in accomplishing these.

So, for example, let's say a leader wants to incorporate the organizational values into the performance management system, but key leaders are reticent about doing so for several reasons. First, while the organization may want to incorporate values development into their strategic planning initiative, this is not scheduled to begin for another 12 months. Second, while the performance appraisal system may be under consideration for overhaul by the human resources department, this will not be ready for another six months. Third, training may need to occur for everyone on this new performance appraisal method, which is beyond the job parameters of any one leader. Therefore, a possible "baby step" a leader may take is to tell everyone that he/she intends to incorporate these values into all performance discussions he/she will have with direct reports.

OBSTACLES THAT CAN GET IN THE WAY OF ACTION

As with any potential new action, our own behaviors can get in the way of forward movement. These obstacles can prevent us from being successful and, subsequently, bring about what I call "learned apathy"—this action hasn't worked previously so there is nothing more I can do. Obviously, this is tantamount to remaining in a status quo "rut." So, I believe it is important to recognize some of the obstacles that can get in the way. By being cognizant of these and spotting the road signs along the way, we can be better prepared to handle these roadblocks. Table 9.3 identifies some of the top obstacles.

TABLE 9.3

How Status Quo Thinking Can Present Obstacles That Get in the Way of Taking Action

- "It's been this way for a long time and it will never change."
- "I've tried this before with no positive outcome."
- "Look at what happened to my peer; she got berated for trying to confront the toxic person."
- "The toxic person wields too much power for me to do anything."
- "It's just a matter of time before someone else gets wise to his toxic ways."
- "My boss will never support me in trying to confront this person."
- "It's just a losing battle. I'd better leave well enough alone."

BUILDING A CULTURE OF EVERYDAY CIVILITY ONE ACTION AT A TIME

I cannot emphasize enough the power of sharing your results with others, as appropriate and relevant. Gather their thoughts into your action plan, into ways to improve it, and its viability. These kinds of discussions spread everyday civility concepts like a proactive virus. And as one action is completed, tackle others—particularly those that are more difficult.

Also, incorporated within this book is the power of one of my mantras: *To be a leader is to teach. If you're not teaching, you're not leading.* Therefore, discuss these concepts and practices at your staff meetings. Talk about them with your boss. And if your organization has a skip-level discussion process in place, address some of these with your boss's boss!

It takes a village. And all these actions help build everyday civility capacity *and* help create a culture where there is less likelihood that someone is going to get away with bad behavior. No one person can accomplish achieving a culture of everyday civility alone. "Baby steps" mount to "walking steps" that mount to "quantum leaps." As leadership guru Rosabeth Moss Kanter has noted: Successful organizational change is first about combining short-term "bold strokes" to respond quickly; to catalyze change, it is a "long march" to change systems and habitual behaviors (Kanter, 2004). How will you combine short-term approaches with a long-term march towards everyday civility?

This book has hopefully helped you determine how to engage both perspectives—long-term strategy with short-term wins—through its many cases, examples, templates, and spontaneous self-completion inventories. Changing simple behaviors, teaching others what and why you are doing this, and gradually tackling longer-term strategies will put you on the road to your organization or team being in an everyday civility zone. With this being practiced by everyone, everyday civility will become your new organizational mantra.

I cannot emphasize enough the power of sharing your results with others, as appropriate and relevant. Gather their thoughts into your action plan, into ways to improve it, and its viability, ensuring that it can be accomplished. These kinds of discussions spread everyday civility concepts like a proactive virus.

References

Borysenko, K. (2015, April 22). What was management thinking? The high cost of employee turnover. *Talent Management and HR.*

Campbell, D. P., & Hallam, G. (1994). Campbell-Hallam Team Development Survey™, Chicago: General Dynamics.

careerbuilder.com (April 20, 2011). One-in-four workers have felt bullied in the workplace.

Cortina, L. M., Magley, V. J., Williams, J. H., & Langhout, R. D. (2001). Incivility in the workplace: Incidence and impact. *Journal of Occupational Health Psychology, 6* (1), 64–80.

Fernandez-Araoz, C., Groysberg, B., & Nohria, N. (2009, May). The definitive guide to recruiting in good times and bad. *Harvard Business Review, 87* (5), 74–84.

Fisher, R., & Ury, W. (1981). *Getting to yes: Negotiate without giving in.* New York: Penguin Books.

Kanter, R. M. (2004, December 13). How leaders create winning streaks. *Harvard Business School Working Knowledge.*

Klein, A. S., & Forni, P. M. (2011, July). Barbers of civility. *Archives of Surgery, 146* (7), 774–777.

Kusy, M., & Essex, L. (2005). *Breaking the code of silence: Prominent leaders reveal how they rebounded from seven critical mistakes.* Lanham, MD: Taylor Trade Publishing/ Rowman and Littlefield.

Kusy, M., & Holloway, E. (2009). *Toxic workplace! Managing toxic personalities and their systems of power.* San Francisco, CA: Jossey-Bass.

Kusy, M., & Holloway, E. (2014, March–April). A field guide to real-time culture change. Just "rolling out" a training program just won't cut it. *Journal of Medical Practice Management, 29* (5), 294–303.

Nekoranec, W., & Kusy, M. (2005). Engaging executives in strategic conversations: More than a random event. *OD Practitioner, 37* (4), 20–25.

NSI Nursing Solutions Inc. (2016). 2016 National Healthcare Retention and RN Staffing Report. East Petersburg, PA: NSI Nursing Solutions, Inc.

Pearson, C., & Porath, C. (2009). *The cost of bad behavior.* New York: Penguin Books.

Porath, C., MacInnis, D., & Folkes, V. (2010, August). Witnessing incivility among employees: Effects on consumer anger and negative inferences about companies. *Journal of Consumer Research, 37,* 292–303.

Rosenstein, A. (2002). Nurse-physician relationship: Impact on nurse satisfaction and retention. *American Journal of Nursing, 102* (6), 26–34.

Rosenstein, A. (2010). Measuring and managing the economic impact of disruptive behaviors in the hospital. *Journal of Healthcare Risk Management, 30* (2), 20–26.

Rosenstein, A., & O'Daniel, M. (2005). Disruptive behavior and clinical outcomes: Perceptions of nurses and physicians. *American Journal of Nursing, 105* (1), 54–64.

Rosenstein, A., & O'Daniel, M. (2008). A survey of the impact of disruptive behavior and communication defects on patient safety. *Joint Commission Journal of Quality Patient Safety, 34* (8), 464–471.

Index

A

Actions difficult to implement, 115
Apology, power of, 13–15
Awareness-generating feedback, 59

B

"Backstabbing," 5
Boss feedback strategy, 44–47
Bullying, 9–10

C

Campbell-Hallam Team Development
    Survey™ (TDS), 89, 94, *see also*
    Team assessment method,
    powerful
    case simulation of, 94–98
    description of, 90
    differences between traditional culture
        assessment tools and, 102
    hard data collection using, 95
    how to best engage, 101
    nursing team using, 97
    summary report, 91
    summary of what a sample team
        experiences using, 94
    team culture process and, 98
    360-team process, 100
Candidate interviews, analyzing responses
    from, 71–73
"Catastrophizing" a situation, 48
Chameleons, toxic people as, 1, 3, 26, 88
Civility, *see* Everyday civility, building a
    culture of
Confidant, key questions in finding, 64
Conversation avoidance behaviors,
    49–50
Cost-benefit feedback strategy, 36–38
Culture of everyday civility,
    see Everyday civility, building
    a culture of

D

Declines in performance, 8
Direct report feedback strategy, 38–42
Domains of toxic behaviors, 5

E

Everyday civility, building a culture of,
    113–118
    actions difficult to implement, 115
    building a culture one action at a time,
        118
    checklist of top actions for dealing
        with toxic behaviors, 116
    obstacles, 117
    prioritizing your actions, 115–117
    problem, action, and expected
        outcome, 113–115
    status quo thinking, 117
Evidence-based insights about toxic
    behaviors, 1–15
    apology, power of, 13–15
    "backstabbing," 5
    bullying, 9–10
    chameleons, toxic people as, 1, 3
    declines in performance, 8
    definition and categories of toxic
        behavior, 5–6
    domains of toxic behaviors, 5
    exercise, 10, 11
    financial outcome, 6
    hard data that become a call to action,
        6–8
    high performers, understanding toxic
        people who are, 9
    passive hostility, 5
    quiz, 12
    sabotage, 5
    shaming, 5
Exiting practices, *see* Practices addressing
    toxic behaviors, hiring and exiting
Expertise protector, 55

F

Feedback
  awareness-generating, 59
  false myth of, 27–28
  360-degree, 109–111
Feedback, ways of giving (to toxic people),
    35–51
  boss strategy, 44–47
  "catastrophizing" a situation, 48
  conversation avoidance behaviors, 49–50
  cost-benefit strategy, 36–38
  direct report strategy, 38–42
  feedback conversation enders, 51
  feedback conversation starters, 50
  mixing and matching of strategies, 48–51
  peer strategy, 42–44
  strategy types, 36
Firing protocols, 86–88

G

Gossip, 30, 61
"Groupthink," 72
"Gut feeling," 65

H

Hard data collection, 95
Hiring practices, *see* Practices addressing
    toxic behaviors, hiring
    and exiting
Hypothetical questions, danger of, 69–71

I

Ignoring a toxic person, downward spiral
    of, 26
Interviewing questions, varying of, 73

K

"Knock down and kiss up" action, 3,
    66–67, 103

M

Mentor, benefit of working with, 32
"Mixed-methods" approach (performance
    management), 84

Motivation of toxic buffer, 56–58
Myths about toxic behaviors, 17–34
  (#1) you can't calculate the financial
      cost of toxic people, 17–24
  (#2) many toxic people are
      incompetent, 24–25
  (#3) ignoring the toxic person will stop
      the behavior, 25–26
  (#4) concrete feedback will
      handle their manipulations,
      27–28
  (#5) making up your mind you won't
      put up with toxic behaviors is
      enough, 29–31
  (#6) there's little you can do if your
      boss is toxic, 31–32
  (#7) keeping the problem to yourself
      will protect you in the long run,
      32–34
  chameleons, toxic people as, 26
  generic template, 23
  gossip, 30
  mentor, benefit of working with, 32
  "nearsightedness," 27
  reinforcement theory, 25
  replacement costs (people who quit),
      20
  scenarios, 22
  "secondary gain," 29
  statistics, 19

N

National Healthcare Retention & RN
    Staffing Report, 23
"Nearsightedness," 27
Non-hypothetical questions, 70, 71

P

Passive hostility, 5
Peer feedback strategy, 42–44
Performance management, failures and
    triumphs of, 79–88
  accountability, 81
  chameleons, toxic people as, 88
  discussion, 81
  integration, 81
  "mixed-methods" approach, 84

performance management template,
83–85
powerful performance management
practices, 81–83
protocol for firing the toxic person,
86–88
sample discussion, preparation for,
82–83
70-30 split performance model, 85–86
values integration as antidote to toxic
behaviors, 80–81
Persistence of toxic behaviors, 53–64
awareness, 56
coaching conversation (sample), 61–63
confidant, key questions in finding, 64
expertise protector, 55
getting out of being stuck, 63–64
if someone else is a toxic protector or
buffer, 60–63
if you are a toxic protector or buffer,
59–60
motivation of toxic buffer, 56–58
productivity protector, 54
quiz, 57, 58
social relationship protector, 54
toxic protectors and toxic buffers,
53–56
Practices addressing toxic behaviors,
hiring and exiting, 65–77
candidate interviews, analyzing
responses from, 71–73
checking references, 74–75
data generated from exit interview, 77
exit interview, 65, 76
"groupthink," 72
"gut feeling," 65
hiring manager, 67
hypothetical questions, danger of,
69–71
interviewing questions, varying of, 73
non-hypothetical questions, 70, 71
poorly managed recruiting process,
66–67
recruiting cue sheet, 67–69
scenario, 66
when traditional exit interviews do not
work, 75–77
Problem-action-outcome matrix, 114
Productivity protector, 54

Q

Quiz
toxic buffer, 58
toxic person, 12
toxic protector, 57

R

Recruiting cue sheet, 67–69, *see also*
Practices addressing toxic
behaviors, hiring and exiting
Reinforcement theory, 25
Replacement costs (people who quit), 20

S

Sabotage, 5
"Secondary gain," 29, 100
70-30 split performance model, 85–86
Shaming, 5
Skip-level discussions, 104–106
case example, 106–109
components of, 105
360-degree feedback, 109–111
Social relationship protector, 54
Statistics, toxic people and turnover, 19
Status quo thinking, 117

T

Team assessment method, powerful,
89–102
case simulation of the Campbell-
Hallam Team Development
Survey™, 94–98
differences between the Campbell-
Hallam Team Development
Survey™ and traditional culture
assessment tools, 102
how to best engage the Campbell-
Hallam Team Development
Survey™, 101
"secondary gain," 100
target goals, 96
team decisions, 96
what happens when the team leader is
toxic, 99–101
360-degree feedback, 109–111
Toxic buffer, 55–56

V

Values integration, 80–81
Vigilance, 103–111
    case example of skip-level
        conversation, 106–109
    "knock down kiss up" action, 103
    one-on-one meetings, adequacy of,
        103–104
    skip-level discussions, 104–106
    360-degree feedback, comparing the
        skip-level discussion with,
        109–111